CEFR A1-A2

FRAMEWORK ENGLISH

Colin Thompson   Tim Woolstencroft

KINSEIDO

Kinseido Publishing Co., Ltd.
3-21 Kanda Jimbo-cho, Chiyoda-ku,
Tokyo 101-0051, Japan

First published 2024 by Kinseido Publishing Co., Ltd.

Design: DAITECH co., ltd.

Acknowledgements

The authors would like to thank the students, teachers and staff at Josai International University for their help during the writing and piloting of Framework English series. In particular, we would like to thank Dr. Kenji Sugibayashi and professor Masato Kurabayashi for their continued support of this project.

A huge debt of thanks is owed to Professor Maria Shiguemi Ichiyama for her invaluable advice and support.

Finally, we would like to express our sincerest thanks to Yukiko Thompson and Nobuko Ito, who provided inspiration, cultural help and language support, not to mention unstinting patience.

CEFR-J wordlist - The CEFR-J Wordlist Version 1.6. Compiled by Yukio Tono, Tokyo University of Foreign Studies. Retrieved from http://www.cefrj.org/download.html#cefrj_wordlist on 01/09/2023.

音声ファイル無料ダウンロード

https://www.kinsei-do.co.jp/download/4200

この教科書で DL 00 の表示がある箇所の音声は、上記 URL または QR コードにて
無料でダウンロードできます。自習用音声としてご活用ください。

▶ PC からのダウンロードをお勧めします。スマートフォンなどでダウンロードされる場合は、
　 ダウンロード前に「解凍アプリ」をインストールしてください。
▶ URL は、検索ボックスではなくアドレスバー (URL 表示欄) に入力してください。
▶ お使いのネットワーク環境によっては、ダウンロードできない場合があります。

 CD 00　左記の表示がある箇所の音声は、教室用 CD (Class Audio CD) に収録されています。

Introduction

Welcome to *Framework English A*. This is book 1 in a series of English language textbooks designed to improve learners' communicative and cognitive skills. Based on the aims and assessment criteria of the Common European Framework of Reference for Languages (CEFR), this book follows CEFR's goals for developing learners' language skills. CEFR's assessment criteria is categorized into proficiency levels (A1-C2), and this action-based book primarily targets A1-A2 levels. Vocabulary has been selected from A1-B2 CEFR-J levels; a CEFR informed word list designed for Asian learners of English. The selected language has been allocated within 6 topic-based modules of personal and social relevance for learners, such as food and fashion. These modules are looked at from international viewpoints so learners can improve their understanding of multiculturalism, and also learn to express their opinions about different cultures.

Each module follows a systematic structure. Learners are first provided with learning goals, followed by a progression of tasks and activities that allow learners to practice and develop communicative and cognitive skills. Each module also provides visual graphic organizers that help learners to extract key information from complex listening and reading texts. Graphic organizers are also used to help students plan and organize their thoughts clearly for productive writing. At the end of each module, learners complete "Can-do" statements which reflect the goals outlined at the start of the module, enabling them to assess their strengths and weaknesses. There are also three review units that consist of research projects where learners answer research questions by collecting and reporting on data using key language features of the modules. In doing so, learners develop important cognitive skills such as analyzing information, reasoning, inferring, and displaying visual data.

The communicative and cognitive skills developed from using *Framework English A* can benefit life-long learning not only in relation to students' English studies, but also other areas of their academic studies, as well as their future careers.

C O N T E N T S

MODULE Outline *Using Framework English A*

Goals Introduces the module and activates learners' L2 resources.

1st Unit   *Unit 1, 3, 6, 8, 11, 13*

 MATCH — Learners complete a picture matching task.

 SCAN — Learners practice scanning for information.

FOCUS — Learners focus on communicative functions.

LISTEN — Learners practice their listening skills by completing picture matching tasks, written texts, as well as organizing and summarizing key information using graphic organizers.

COMMUNICATE — Learners practice their communication skills by completing tasks and activities that use the target language.

2nd Unit   *Unit 2, 4, 7, 9, 12, 14*

 READ — Learners engage in pre-reading activities to activate their topic knowledge, then practice reading topic-based texts, before organizing and summarizing key information using graphic organizers.

 WRITE — Learners develop different writing skills by engaging in vocabulary, grammar and skills-based exercises.

 VOCABULARY — Learners test their knowledge of topic-based CEFR-J vocabulary (A1 - A2 - B1 - B2 - + (No level), by completing vocabulary activities and a crossword..

 LANGUAGE REVIEW — Learners review selected grammar and vocabulary items by completing a series of language exercises.

Self-Check Learners evaluate the knowledge and skills learned from each module using CEFR related can-do descriptors.

Review   *Unit 5, 10, 15*

After completing two modules, learners engage in communicative, research-based projects using key vocabulary from the modules.

MODULE 1

Introductions

GOALS:

 Can you scan for information from introductions?

 Can you introduce yourself and ask personal questions?

 Can you understand people when they introduce themselves?

 Can you ask and answer personal questions about other people?

 Can you read and understand introduction messages?

 Can you write a message introducing yourself?

 Can you understand vocabulary related to introductions?

MATCH

Match the pictures with cards **a ~ e**. Write the letter of the card in the space next to the picture.

1.
card
nationality

2.
card
nationality

3.
card
nationality

4.
card
nationality

5.
card
nationality

a
Michael James

Nurse
Los Angeles
Children's Hospital

b
Kim Wilson

Taxi driver
Liverpool Cars

c
S. A. Cantor

Pilot
Iberian Air

d
Ajay Babu

Computer Specialist
Mumbai Financial Services

e
Kulap Boonmee

Student
Bangkok International
University

SCAN

Where are they from?

A *Scanning for information:* In 4 minutes, scan the texts below to find the key information. Check your answers on the previous page.

🎧 DL 02   💿 CD 02

B Read the texts again and write the nationality of each person in the correct space on the previous page.

1. My name is Michael, but all my friends call me Mike. I'm American. I'm from San Francisco, but I live and work in Los Angeles now. I love kids, and I work as a nurse in a children's hospital. In my free time, I enjoy watching sports. I'm a big fan of basketball and baseball.

2. Nice to meet you. My name is Sofia Ana Cantor. My family name means singer in English. I'm Spanish, and I live in Madrid near the airport. I'm a pilot, and I love flying. I work for an airline in Spain. I think I have the best job in the world.

3.  I'm a taxi driver from Britain. In my free time, I love playing sport and watching movies. I especially like watching animation movies with my family. I live in Liverpool with my two young children, Oliver and Ella. Oh, I forgot to tell you my name, it's Kim Wilson. Nice to meet you.

4. Hi, I'm Kulap. I'm from Thailand. I'm a student at a university in Bangkok. My major is Japanese, and I'm really interested in languages. As well as Thai, I also speak Chinese. In my free time, I'm really into reading Japanese manga and watching Japanese anime. My favorite is Naruto.

5.  I'm from Mumbai in India. I'm a computer specialist. I work for a large company. My name is Ajay. I love playing computer games in my free time, and I also like programming apps for my smart phone. I often stay up late and go online. I don't like getting up early. I'm not a morning person.

C *Introduce yourself:* Include your picture, your name, where you are from and what you do.

FOCUS

A *Introductions:* Match phrases **1-6** with pictures **a-f**.

1. I love watching soccer. ··········· ☐

2. I study Business. ·············· ☐

3. I like listening to music and reading. ☐

4. I'm from California. ············· ☐

5. My name is John. ··············· ☐

6. I live in Kyoto. ··················· ☐

a.

b.

c.

d.

e.

f.

B *Personal questions:* Match questions **7-12** with phrases **1-6**.

7. What's your name? ············· ☐

8. What do you do for fun? ·········· ☐

9. What sports do you like? ·········· ☐

10. Where are you from? ············ ☐

11. Where do you live? ·············· ☐

12. What's your major? ·············· ☐

→ *Think of an extra personal question and write it below:*

_____

C 💬💬 *Let's talk:* In pairs, take turns asking and answering the questions in part B.

For example:

A: What's your name?
B: My name is *Akira*.
A: Where are you from?
B: I'm from *Hokkaido*.

8

LISTEN

 DL 03   CD 03

A Listen to the first part of the conversation. Write the names of the people talking in the box under each picture. Write Y or M-J next to the correct picture to match their nationality, where they live and their interests.

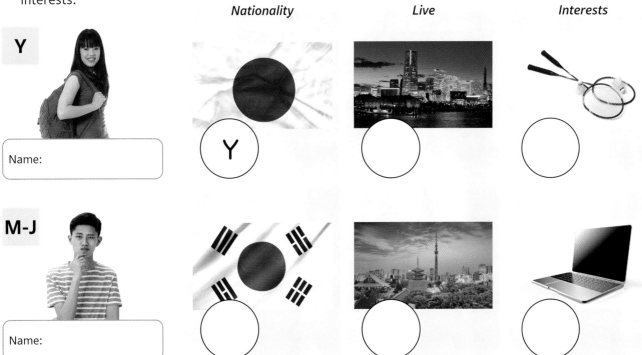

B Read the conversation below and try to guess the missing words. Then listen to the conversation again, check your answers and complete it.

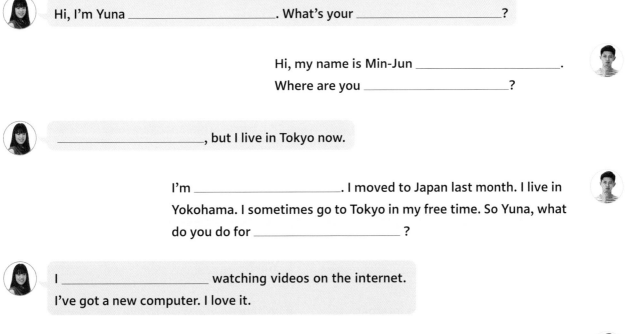

Hi, I'm Yuna _____. What's your _____?

Hi, my name is Min-Jun _____.
Where are you _____?

_____, but I live in Tokyo now.

I'm _____. I moved to Japan last month. I live in Yokohama. I sometimes go to Tokyo in my free time. So Yuna, what do you do for _____?

I _____ watching videos on the internet. I've got a new computer. I love it.

Cool! I'm really into _____. At the moment, I'm playing a lot of _____.

C Now listen to the rest of the conversation and complete the mind map below.

Nationality / Live

Japanese /
Tokyo

Interests

Job

Yuna Saito

Family

Nationality / Live

Interests

Job

Family

D 💬💬 Give your opinion!

1. I want to study abroad in the future.

Agree: _____   Disagree: _____

Why? _____

2. I enjoy watching videos on the internet.

Agree: _____   Disagree: _____

Why? _____

3. I'm not into sports.

Agree: _____   Disagree: _____

Why? _____

4. Where do you want to live after you graduate?

Answer: _____

Why? _____

COMMUNICATE   Who am I? (A)

In pairs, student (A) looks at the cards on this page, student (B) looks at the cards on the next page.
Ask questions to find the missing information and fill out the cards on the right.

Example: B(1a): "What country is she from?" A(1a): "She's from Norway."

1a

Name: Astrid Larsen
Country: Norway
Home: Oslo
Job: Police officer
Birthday: September 3
Interests: Skiing

1b

Name:
Country:
Home:
Job:
Birthday:
Interests:

2a

Name: Siti Aziz
Country: Malaysia
Home: Kuala Lumpur
Job: Elementary school teacher
Birthday: August 2
Interests: Taking photographs

2b

Name:
Country:
Home:
Job:
Birthday:
Interests:

3b

Name:
Country:
Home:
Job:
Birthday:
Interests:

3a

Name: Zoe Campbell
Country: Canada
Home: Toronto
Job: High school student
Birthday: February 14
Interests: Painting

COMMUNICATE
Who am I? (B)

In pairs, student (B) looks at the cards on this page, student (A) looks at the cards on the previous page.
Ask questions to find the missing information and fill out the cards on the left.

Example: A(1b): "What country is he from?" B(1b): "He's from France."

1a
Name:
Country:
Home:
Job:
Birthday:
Interests:

1b
Name: Michel Blanc
Country: France
Home: Lyon
Job: Writer
Birthday: March 11
Interests: Playing the guitar

2a
Name:
Country:
Home:
Job:
Birthday:
Interests:

2b
Name: Seojun Choi
Country: Korea
Home: Incheon
Job: Lawyer
Birthday: December 20
Interests: Shopping

3a
Name:
Country:
Home:
Job:
Birthday:
Interests:

3b
Name: Martin Garcia
Country: Argentina
Home: Buenos Aires
Job: Retired
Birthday: July 21
Interests: Dancing (tango)

UNIT **2**

READ / WRITE / VOCABULARY / LANGUAGE REVIEW

READ   Self-introductions

A *Brainstorm:* First, think of three personal questions and answers.

For example: name, hometown, interests

1. Q _____

    A _____

2. Q _____

    A _____

3. Q _____

    A _____

B *Pre-reading:*

  1. Complete questions **a-f**.

  2. Look at the picture above, try to guess the answers to the questions and write them down.

  3. Read the message on next page and check your answers.

  a. What _____ her name?

    _____ _____
    (Your answer)   (Correct answer)

  b. Where _____ she from?

    _____ _____
    (Your answer)   (Correct answer)

  c. Where _____ she live?

    _____ _____
    (Your answer)   (Correct answer)

  d. What _____ she do?

    _____ _____
    (Your answer)   (Correct answer)

  e. What sport _____ she like?

    _____ _____
    (Your answer)   (Correct answer)

  f. What _____ she do for fun?

    _____ _____
    (Your answer)   (Correct answer)

C Read the student's self-introduction message. Then complete the mind map below.

Hi everyone,

My name's Andrea Smith. My friends call me Andi. I'm from Seattle, but I live in New York. I'm twenty years old, and I'm a student at a university there. I'm a Business major. I live in a small apartment near the university, and I work part-time at a fast food restaurant near my apartment.

My family lives in Seattle. My father is a businessman. He works for an IT company. My mother is a homemaker, and she also does volunteer work at a hospital in her free time. I have an older brother and a younger sister. My brother is studying Law in Los Angeles, and my sister is a high school student in Seattle.

In my free time, I'm into playing basketball and watching movies with my friends. I also like listening to music online and reading comic books. I love staying up late on weekends. I'm not a morning person!
Best,
Andi

Introduction
(Her hometown, where she lives and what she does)

- From Seattle
- Lives in New York

Andrea "Andi" Smith

Family

Free time & interests

WRITE — Self-introductions

A *Word check:* Complete this student's self-introduction. Use words from the vocabulary box below to help you.

Hi everyone. My _____ is James Field. My _____ call me Jim. I'm nineteen _____ old and I'm _____ Sydney. I'm a _____ at a university in Osaka. My _____ is Japanese. I have a _____ job. I _____ at a restaurant.

My parents _____ in Sydney. My _____ is a police officer. He works very hard. My _____ is a high school teacher. She likes her job. I don't _____ any brothers or sisters. I'm an _____ child.

In my free time, I like _____ tennis and _____ to music. I play tennis two or three times a week at university. I practice from 6:00 p.m. to 8:00 p.m. I listen to rock music every day. I'm also into watching my _____ bands on the internet.

favorite	listening	work	major	part-time	live	have	from
friends	name	playing	father	student	mother	only	years

B *Writing skill:* Writing main ideas with supporting details.

- Writing main ideas with supporting details.
  For example: *My family lives in Tokyo.*
- Supporting details then provide extra information **about the topic**.
  For example: ◯ *My father is a doctor.*
  ✕ *My favorite food is pizza.*

C *Let's practice!:* Write a main idea followed by supporting details about:

You : Write your name, where you are from, and where you live and what you do.

My name is _____. I'm from _____.

I live in _____. I'm a _____.

Your family or friends : Where they live and what they do.

My family lives / friends live in _____. I have / don't have any

_____.

Your free time and interests : What you do in your free time and what you are interested in.

In my free time, I like _____.

D *TASK:* Write notes on your self-introduction below using the examples and details above. Write about the topics on the right:

Introduction
(Your hometown, what you do and where you live)

Family & friends
(Where they live and what they do)

Free time & interests
(What you do in your free time and what you are interested in)

VOCABULARY

🎧 DL 06   💿 CD 06

Adjectives

comic *A2* ....

favorite *A1* ....

interested *A1* ....

new *A1* ....

old(er) *A1* ....

online *A1* ....

part-time *B1* ....

young(er) *A1* ....

Adverbs

abroad *A2* ....

late *A1* ....

online *A2* ....

part-time *B1* ....

really *A1* ....

well *A1* ....

Nouns

baseball *A1* ....

birthday *A1* ....

blood *A2* type *A1* ....

brother *A1* ....

country *A2* ....

father *A1* ....

free *A1* time *A1* ....

friend *A1* ....

(the) future *A1* ....

interest *A2* ....

job *A1* ....

major *B2* ....

morning *A1* ....

movie(s) *A1* ....

music *A1* ....

nurse *A1* ....

person *A1* ....

mother *A1* ....

only *A1* child *A1* ....

parent *A1* ....

sister *A1* ....

student *A1* ....

swimming *A1* ....

university *A2* ....

video game(s) *A2* ....

Verbs

be into *+* ....

enjoy *A1* ....

graduate *A2* ....

hang out *+* (with friends *A1*) ....

listen *A1* (to music *A1*) ....

play *A1* (video games *A2*)

....

read *A1* (comic *A2* books *A1*)

....

stay up *+* (late *A1*) ....

study *A1* (abroad *A2*) ....

watch *A1* movies *A1* ....

A Match each definition with the words on the right.

1. A popular ball game in America: _____ **a.** student
2. Someone who studies at university: _____ **b.** friend
3. Someone you like a lot: _____ **c.** be into
4. To like something: _____ **d.** baseball

B Choose the correct words from the box that best complete the questions. Answer the questions.

fun	do	from	blood	into

1. What do you [_____]?

   Your answer: _____

2. What is your [_____] type?

   Your answer: _____

3. What do you do for [_____]?

   Your answer: _____

4. Where are you [_____]?

   Your answer: _____

5. Are you [_____] horror movies?

   Your answer: _____

C *Crossword:* Complete the crossword using the hints below.

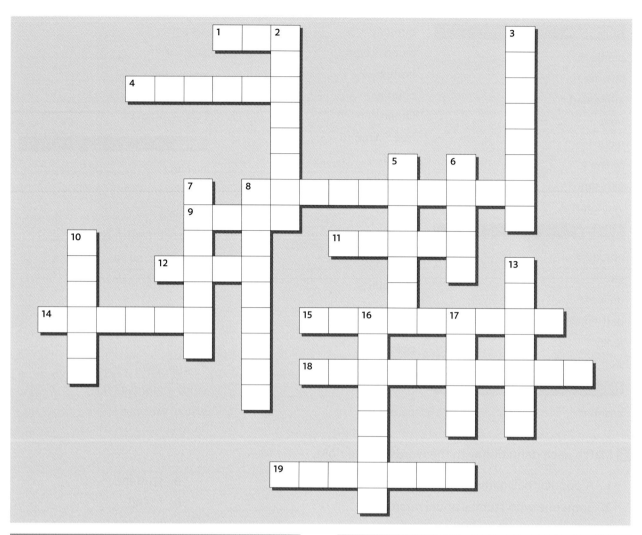

Across

1. Do you have a part-time _____ ?

4.   8.

9. I'm an _____ child.

11. Do you like playing _____ games?

12. I'm really _____ surfing at the moment.

14.   15. I really like _____ to music. I love J-pop.

18.   19. I don't like getting up early.

   I'm not a _____ person.

Down

2.   3.   5.

6. My _____ is Business.

7. What _____ are you from? France.

8.   10. I want to study _____ in Canada.

13. On weekends, I enjoy _____ out with friends.

1    17.

18

LANGUAGE REVIEW

Asking and answering personal questions

Present tense Wh- questions (Be verb)	
When is your birthday?	My birthday is June 2nd.
What's your major?	My major is Business.
What country are you from?	I'm from Spain.

Present tense Wh- questions (Other verbs)	
Where do you live?	I live in Fukuoka.
Where does she live?	She lives in Madrid.
Where does he live?	He lives in Los Angeles.

Yes/No questions (Be verb)	
Is your birthday in May?	No, it isn't. It's in June.
Are you from India?	No, I'm not. I'm from Sri Lanka.
Is she from Japan?	Yes, she is. She's from Sendai.

Yes/No questions (Other verbs)	
Do you live in Kumamoto?	No, I don't. I live in Kagoshima.
Does she live near here?	Yes, she lives near the station.
Does he live in China?	Yes, he does. He lives in Dalian.

A Put the questions in the correct order and answer them.

1. [music / like / you / do / what] ? ▶ _____?

   Your answer: _____

2. [major / your / is / what] ? ▶ _____?

   Your answer: _____

3. [the / you / near / live / do / university] ? ▶ _____?

   Your answer: _____

4. [from / teacher / is / your / Japan] ? ▶ _____?

   Your answer: _____

5. [you / sports / play / what / do] ? ▶ _____?

   Your answer: _____

B Choose a, b, c or d.

1. My birthday _____ January 2nd.
   a. is **b.** are **c.** do **d.** does

2. Where is _____ English teacher from?
   a. you **b.** your **c.** a **d.** has

3. I _____ from England.
   a. does **b.** do **c.** is **d.** am

4. I _____ part-time at a convenience store.
   a. do **b.** am **c.** have **d.** work

5. I live _____ Tokyo.
   a. is **b.** in **c.** a **d.** the

MODULE 1 SELF-CHECK

Write a score (1-5)* in the boxes below to show how well you can do each part of the module. If you can't do any part well, go back to the page and practice again.

* 1 : Not at all   **2 :** A little   **3 :** OK   **4 :** Well   **5 :** Very well

UNIT 1

🔍 SCAN

I can scan for information about nationalities (p.7). ⸱⸱

🎧 FOCUS

I can introduce myself and ask personal questions (p.8). ⸱⸱⸱⸱⸱⸱⸱⸱⸱⸱⸱⸱⸱⸱⸱⸱⸱⸱⸱⸱⸱⸱⸱⸱⸱⸱⸱⸱⸱⸱⸱

👂 LISTEN

I can understand people when they introduce themselves (p.9-10). ⸱⸱⸱⸱⸱⸱⸱⸱⸱⸱⸱⸱⸱⸱⸱⸱⸱⸱⸱⸱

👥 COMMUNICATE

I can ask and answer personal questions about other people (p.11-12). ⸱⸱⸱⸱⸱⸱⸱⸱⸱⸱⸱⸱⸱⸱⸱⸱⸱⸱⸱⸱

UNIT 2

📖 READ

I can read and understand introduction messages (p.13-14). ⸱⸱⸱⸱⸱⸱⸱⸱⸱⸱⸱⸱⸱⸱⸱⸱⸱⸱⸱⸱⸱⸱⸱⸱⸱⸱⸱

✍️ WRITE

I can write a message introducing myself (p.15-16). ⸱⸱⸱⸱⸱⸱⸱⸱⸱⸱⸱⸱⸱⸱⸱⸱⸱⸱⸱⸱⸱⸱⸱⸱⸱⸱⸱⸱⸱⸱⸱⸱⸱

💬 VOCABULARY

I can understand vocabulary related to introductions (p.17-18). ⸱⸱⸱⸱⸱⸱⸱⸱⸱⸱⸱⸱⸱⸱⸱⸱⸱⸱⸱⸱⸱⸱⸱

MODULE 2

Fashion

GOALS:

 Can you scan for information about fashion styles?

 Can you describe your fashion interests?

 Can you understand conversations about clothes?

 Can you find out about your classmates' fashion styles?

 Can you read and understand people's opinions about fashion?

 Can you write your opinion about the clothes you like?

 Can you understand vocabulary related to fashion?

UNIT 3

MATCH

Match decades **1-5** with fashion pictures **a-e** below.

SCAN

 DL 07   CD 07

A *Scanning for information:* In 4 minutes, scan the text below to find the key information.
Check your answers on the previous page.

1. The Beatles are the most famous group in the world in the sixties, and their fashion is also very popular. Men are into mod fashion and are wearing dark suits with black ties and Chelsea boots. For girls, miniskirts are stylish, and short hair is popular.

2. Disco music is cool in the 1970s. Flared jeans and platform shoes with high heels are in fashion. By the end of the 70s, teenagers are wearing unique styles called punk fashion and listening to punk rock music. People have their hair cut in strange Mohican styles that are dyed in bright colors.

3. Going back to the eighties, we can see lots of designer brands and loose suits for both men and women. People like wearing suits in different colors and often wear them with T-shirts. Jackets have big shoulder designs, and women wear tight skirts. This is called yuppie fashion.

4.  In the 1990s, hip-hop is the latest fashion. People wear loose, baggy jeans, extra-large T-shirts and work boots or basketball sneakers. Also, baseball caps and hooded tops are popular. Bright-colored sports clothes are fashionable for young people.

5. It is a new millennium and hipster fashion is the new craze. A lot of men have beards and tattoos. Tight jeans and checked shirts are trendy, and both women and men wear skater-style clothes. T-shirts and knitted caps are in fashion, and used clothing is really popular.

B In pairs, discuss which decade's fashion you like the best. Also describe the clothes you are wearing now and what kind of fashion styles you like.

For example: *I like 90's fashion the best. I think baggy jeans and large T-shirts look cool.*

FOCUS

A *Fashion expressions:* Match phrases **1-8** with pictures **a-h** below.

1. tight jeans · · · · · · · · · · · · · · · · · · · [ ]

2. dyed hair · [ ]

3. tattoos · [ ]

4. bright-colored sneakers · · · · · · · · · [ ]

5. school uniforms · · · · · · · · · · · · · · [ ]

6. loose clothes · · · · · · · · · · · · · · · · [ ]

7. beards · [ ]

8. designer bags · · · · · · · · · · · · · · · [ ]

a.

b.

c.

d.

e.

f.

g.

h.

B *Likes and dislikes:* Mark the phrases below with positive, negative or neutral images.

I love... [☺☺]

I'm really into... [ ]

I can't stand... [ ]

I'm not into... [ ]

... look(s) cool [ ]

... look(s) stylish [ ]

... look(s) bad [ ]

... is/are O.K. [ ]

like

dislike

C *Let's talk:* In pairs, discuss your fashion interests. Use the phrases from **A** and **B**. Make sure you agree or disagree with reasons.

For example:

A: Do you like dyed hair?
B: Yes, I think dyed hair looks cool.
A: Really? I'm not into dyed hair. I like natural hair.

LISTEN

A conversation about clothes

 DL 08   CD 08

A Listen to the conversation. Write the names of the people talking in the box under each picture. Then write C or G next to the correct picture to match the clothes they are wearing to the party.

	Tops	*Bottoms*	*Footwear*

C

Name:

G

Name:

B Read the same conversation below and try to guess the missing words. Then listen to the conversation again, check your answers and complete it below.

 Hi. What are you _____?

I'm _____ ready for the party tonight.

 Me too. I'm _____ in about twenty minutes.

What are you _____?

 I'm not wearing anything _____. My new green skirt and a denim jacket. They go well together. And I'm wearing sneakers. I don't like wearing high heels at parties.

Great. I'm wearing _____ clothes, too. I'm wearing a black hoody and a pair of old _____. I decided not to wear sneakers. I'm wearing the black _____ that I bought last week.

 Good idea. I think they look really _____.

C Now listen to the full conversation, and circle the clothes that the two are wearing for the party and at work.

C _____   G _____

Party

Work

D 💬💬 Give your opinion!

1. I'm not interested in fashion.

  Agree: _____   Disagree: _____

  Why? _____

2. I prefer tight jeans to loose jeans.

  Agree: _____   Disagree: _____

  Why? _____

3. I think used clothes look cool.

  Agree: _____   Disagree: _____

  Why? _____

4. I think uniforms are a good idea.

  Agree: _____   Disagree: _____

  Why? _____

COMMUNICATE

How well do you know your classmates' fashion styles?

A Look at sentences **1~10** below. Write the name of a different classmate you think fits each number. Then write the question so that you check the answers with the students.

B Ask each student and, if you are correct, mark "o" in the box. If you are wrong, mark "x" in the box. If possible, ask extra questions and make notes.

Your guess / Question / Extra information	Result
1. *I guess _____ is really interested in fashion.* Q: _____ Extra information : _____	
2. *I guess _____ likes striped shirts more than plain shirts.* Q: _____ Extra information : _____	
3. *I guess _____ enjoys shopping in the January sales.* Q: _____ Extra information : _____	
4. *I guess _____ has a designer bag or wallet.* Q: _____ Extra information : _____	
5. *I guess _____ has more than 5 pairs of shoes.* Q: _____ Extra information : _____	
6. *I guess _____ is going shopping for clothes this weekend.* Q: _____ Extra information : _____	
7. *I guess _____ is wearing something new.* Q: _____ Extra information : _____	
8. *I guess _____ hates wearing formal clothes.* Q: _____ Extra information : _____	
9. *I guess _____ isn't into wearing bright colors.* Q: _____ Extra information : _____	
10. *I guess _____ prefers used clothes to new ones.* Q: _____ Extra information : _____	

READ / WRITE / VOCABULARY / LANGUAGE REVIEW

READ

Opinions about fashion

A *Brainstorm:* What clothes do you like wearing in summer / winter?

For example: In summer, I usually wear ... / In winter, I like wearing ...

B *Pre-reading:* Match the pictures with comments **a-l** below.

a. I have a really cute designer bag.

b. I'm wearing a checked shirt.

c. I like wearing rubber sandals. I don't think they are stylish, but they are comfortable.

d. In winter, I like wearing hoodies in bright colors.

e. I go surfing a lot, so I often wear beach shorts.

f. When I'm at work, I always wear a formal business suit.

g. Today it's so cold, so I'm wearing my down vest.

h. I think striped T-shirts are cool.

i. At Christmas, I always wear my favorite sweater. It's red with a funny reindeer design.

j. I like wearing ripped jeans because they are fashionable.

k. My favorite jacket is my leather jacket.

l. I love wearing my pink sneakers because they go well with my jeans.

DL 10   CD 10

C Two people are talking about fashion. Read their comments and complete the information **1-8** below.

A Kei

In summer, I usually wear casual clothes. I go surfing a lot, so I often wear beach shorts. I always wear T-shirts when it is hot. I think striped T-shirts are cool. I like them more than plain T-shirts. At the beach, I like wearing rubber sandals. I don't think they are stylish, but they are comfortable.

In winter, I like wearing hoodies in bright colors. I think my red hoody looks cool. Today it's so cold, so I'm wearing my down vest. I bought it on discount. At Christmas, I always wear my favorite sweater. It's red with a funny reindeer design. I think it's really unique!

FASHION VOICES

When I'm at work, I always wear a formal business suit and high heels. I think formal clothes look smart. My new high heels are not comfortable, but they are stylish. Also, I have a really cute designer bag. It's expensive, but I love it.

B Anna

At home, I like wearing loose clothes. Now, I'm wearing a checked shirt and ripped jeans. I like wearing ripped jeans because they are fashionable. I don't like tight jeans because they don't suit me. My favorite jacket is my leather jacket. I got it at a used clothes store. I don't wear high heels in my free time. I love wearing my pink sneakers because they go well with my jeans.

What? - Write the name of the item of clothing

Who? - Write the name of the person who wears it

When/Where? - Write when (summer/winter) or where (work/home) the person wears the clothes

---

1.

What?
| a business suit |

Who?
| Anna |

When/Where?
| work |

2.

What?

Who?

When/Where?

3.

What?

Who?

When/Where?

4.

What?

Who?

When/Where?

5.

What?

Who?

When/Where?

6.

What?

Who?

When/Where?

7.

What?

Who?

When/Where?

8.

What?

Who?

When/Where?

A *Word check:* Complete the student's opinion on fashion. Use words from the vocabulary box below to help you.

I'm really _____ designer t-shirts! I think they're cool because they're so _____. They are available in different _____. I like wearing designer t-shirts with jeans. I think they _____ me. Today, I'm wearing a black designer t-shirt. I _____ wear this shirt at university.

I also love wearing new sneakers. I think they're great because they feel so _____. I like wearing sneakers with _____ designs. I always wear sneakers at university. The sneakers I'm wearing now are white and red. I like wearing these sneakers in my _____. Some sneakers can be expensive but there are special offers and _____ during sales.

> usually   colors   discounts   different
> suit   into   fashionable   comfortable   free time

B *Writing skill:* Opinion paragraph writing

Opinion paragraph writing is about giving your opinions on a topic. Use expressions such as "I think…" or "I believe…" Also, give reasons or supporting details to provide extra information.

For example: *I think hooded sweatshirts are cool because they look stylish, and lots of students wear them. I like ripped jeans. I think they look good.*

C *Let's Practice:* Complete your answer to the question below by filling in the blanks.

What clothes do you like wearing? Why do you like them? What are you wearing now?(Use words from the Vocabulary page to help you).

→ I think _____ are stylish. I like wearing them because they are _____

_____. Now, I'm wearing _____

_____.

D *Task:* Think of clothes you like, then write about them. Describe the clothes and give reasons why you like them.

Use the space below to plan your writing.

MY FASHION STYLE

VOCABULARY

Adjectives			
bright *A1*	natural *A2*	design *A1*	offer *A2*
casual *B1*	plain *B1*	discount *B1*	style *A2*
checked +	special *A1*	dress *A1*	suit *A2*
colored +	striped +	earring(s) *A2*	sweater *A2*
comfortable *A2*	stylish *B1*	(high) heel(s) *B1*	sweatshirt *B1*
dark *A1*	tight *A1*	jacket *A1*	T-shirt *A1*
designer *B2*	unique *B1*	jeans *A1*	tatoo *B2*
different *A1*	used *A2*	sale *A1*	uniform *A2*
dyed +	**Nouns**	sandal(s) *B1*	vest +
fashionable *B1*	bag *A1*	shirt *A1*	**Verbs**
formal *B1*	beard *B1*	shoe(s) *A1*	prefer *A2*
latest *A2*	boot(s) *B1*	shopping *A1*	(can't) stand +
leather *A2*	cap *A1*	shorts *A2*	suit *A2*
loose *A2*	clothes *A1*	skirt *A1*	wear *A1*
		sneaker(s) +	

A Match each definition with the words on the right.

1. Feels nice: _____   **a.** jeans
2. Clothes worn at school: _____   **b.** cap
3. Something you wear on your head: _____   **c.** uniform
4. Pants made from denim: _____   **d.** comfortable

B Complete **1-4** below using opposites of the words listed.

1. loose   ⟷   _____

2. formal   ⟷   _____

3. natural hair ⟷   _____

4. dark   ⟷   _____

C Choose the words from the box that best complete the questions. Answer the questions.

wearing   think   sneakers   shopping   interested

1. Are you _____ in fashion?   A: _____

2. What do you _____ of uniforms?   A: _____

3. Do you like _____ loose clothes?   A: _____

4. Is your classmate wearing _____ ?   A: _____

5. Do you enjoy _____ for clothes?   A: _____

D *Crossword:* Complete the crossword using the hints below.

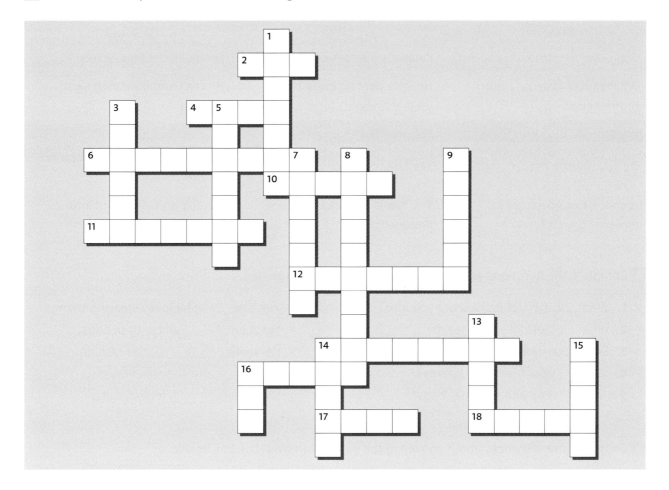

Across

2.

4. I love looking for bargains at _____ clothes stores.

6.

10. I can't _____ wearing ties.

11. I think _____ jackets look cool.

12. My jacket was cheap. It was on _____ offer.

14. I'm really into _____ brands.

16.

17.

18.

Down

1. In the summer, I often wear rubber _____ .

3. Her hair is dyed blue. It looks so _____ .

5.

7. My friend always wears the latest fashions. She is so _____ .

8. My brother isn't _____ in fashion.

9. I like casual clothes more than _____ clothes.

13.

14.

15.

16.

LANGUAGE REVIEW

Questions	Likes	Dislikes
What kind of clothes do you like?	I'm really into designer clothes.	I don't like leather jackets.
What kind of fashion is your brother into?	He likes wearing loose clothes more than tight clothes.	He can't stand wearing tight clothes.

Questions	Likes	Dislikes
Do your friends like tattoos?	Yes, they do. They love tattoos!	No, they don't. They're not into tattoos.
Is your sister interested in designer brands?	Yes, she is. She loves wearing designer clothes.	No, she isn't. She's not into expensive clothes.

A Complete the questions and answers then match them together.

1. What _kind_ of fashion are you into? •
2. What clothes does your teacher _____? •
3. Does your mother _____ earrings? •
4. _____ your friend like beards? •
5. _____ you into designer bags? •

• Yes, she ____. She loves wearing them.
• Yes, I am. I _____ all types of bags.
• I'm really _into_ sixties fashion.
• No, he ____. He shaves every day.
• She usually _____ formal suits.

B Complete the sentences about you using the expression from the box below.

| love   can't stand   don't really like   enjoy   am really into   am not interested in |

1. I _____ going shopping for clothes.
2. I _____ wearing bright colors.
3. I _____ reading about fashion.
4. I _____ buying clothes online.
5. I _____ used clothes designs.
6. I _____ wearing formal clothes.

C Put the questions in the correct order and answer them.

1. [striped / t-shirts / like / do / you]?

   Q._____

   A._____

2. [you / think / do / cool / are / beards]?

   Q._____

   A._____

3. [you / wearing / are / what]?

   Q._____

   A._____

MODULE 2 SELF-CHECK

Write a score (1-5)* in the boxes below to show how well you can do each part of the module. If you can't do any part well, go back to the page and practice again.

* 1 : Not at all   **2 :** A little   **3 :** OK   **4 :** Well   **5 :** Very well

UNIT 3

SCAN
I can scan for information about fashion styles (p.23). ⋯⋯⋯⋯⋯⋯⋯⋯ ☐

FOCUS
I can describe my fashion interests (p.24). ⋯⋯⋯⋯⋯⋯⋯⋯⋯⋯ ☐

LISTEN
I can understand a conversation about clothes (p.25-26). ⋯⋯⋯⋯⋯ ☐

COMMUNICATE
I can find out about my classmates' fashion styles (p.27). ⋯⋯⋯⋯ ☐

UNIT 4

READ
I can read and understand people's opinions about fashion (p.28-29). ⋯⋯⋯ ☐

WRITE
I can write my opinion about the clothes I like (p.30-31). ⋯⋯⋯ ☐

VOCABULARY
I can understand vocabulary related to fashion (p.32-33). ⋯⋯⋯⋯ ☐

PROJECT A

What do you know about your classmates?

First, write the correct questions below. Then ask 10 classmates and mark their answers in the tables below.

1. How many classmates are NOT from the east of Japan?

Q	*Are you from the east of Japan? or Where are you from?*

From the east of Japan (Number)	Not from the east of Japan (Number)	From the east of Japan (%)	Not from the east of Japan (%)

2. How many classmates have B blood type?

Q	

Have B blood type (Number)	Don't have B blood type (Number)	Have B blood type (%)	Don't have B blood type (%)

3. How many classmates have a pet?

Q	

Have a pet (Number)	Don't have a pet (Number)	Have a pet (%)	Don't have a pet (%)

4. How many classmates play a musical instrument?

Q	

Play a musical instrument (Number)	Don't play a musical instrument (Number)	Play a musical instrument (%)	Don't play a musical instrument (%)

5. How many classmates live near the university?

Q	

Live near the university (Number)	Don't live near the university (Number)	Live near the university (%)	Don't live near the university (%)

RESULTS

Draw pie charts using the data from the previous page.

1. How many classmates are NOT from the east of Japan?

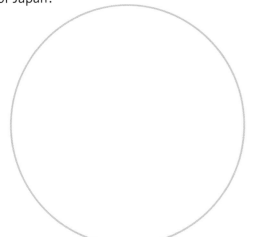

2. How many classmates have B blood type?

3. How many classmates have a pet?

4. How many classmates play a musical instrument?

5. How many classmates live near the university?

REPORT

Write the results of your survey.

Eight students in my group are from the east of Japan. Only four students have a pet.....

PRESENTATION

Take turns explaining the results of your survey to your classmates using the pie charts in the previous page.

PROJECT B

Do students have similar fashion styles?

Ask 10 classmates (5 males and 5 females, if possible) to give their opinion on **1-5** below. Then, note their answers and add their total scores and average in the tables below.

For example:

	Strongly agree (5 points)	Agree (4 points)	It depends (3 points)	Disagree (2 points)	Strongly disagree (1 point)	Total	Average
M			/ / /	/	/	12	2.4
F	/ /	/ / /				22	2.4

1. I usually wear designer clothes.

	Strongly agree (5 points)	Agree (4 points)	It depends (3 points)	Disagree (2 points)	Strongly disagree (1 point)	Total	Average
M							
F							

2. I can't stand wearing uniforms.

	Strongly agree (5 points)	Agree (4 points)	It depends (3 points)	Disagree (2 points)	Strongly disagree (1 point)	Total	Average
M							
F							

3. I rarely dye my hair.

	Strongly agree (5 points)	Agree (4 points)	It depends (3 points)	Disagree (2 points)	Strongly disagree (1 point)	Total	Average
M							
F							

4. I love loose clothes.

	Strongly agree (5 points)	Agree (4 points)	It depends (3 points)	Disagree (2 points)	Strongly disagree (1 point)	Total	Average
M							
F							

5. I'm not into tattoos.

	Strongly agree (5 points)	Agree (4 points)	It depends (3 points)	Disagree (2 points)	Strongly disagree (1 point)	Total	Average
M							
F							

RESULTS

Draw column charts showing your data from the previous page by filling in the blanks below.

SA=Strongly Agree A=Agree ID=It Depends D=Disagree SD=Strongly Agree

1. I usually wear designer clothes.

Group 1				
5				
4				
3				
2				
1				
SA	A	ID	D	SD

Group 2				
5				
4				
3				
2				
1				
SA	A	ID	D	SD

2. I can't stand wearing uniforms.

Group 1				
5				
4				
3				
2				
1				
SA	A	ID	D	SD

Group 2				
5				
4				
3				
2				
1				
SA	A	ID	D	SD

3. I rarely dye my hair.

Group 1				
5				
4				
3				
2				
1				
SA	A	ID	D	SD

Group 2				
5				
4				
3				
2				
1				
SA	A	ID	D	SD

4. I love loose clothes.

Group 1				
5				
4				
3				
2				
1				
SA	A	ID	D	SD

Group 2				
5				
4				
3				
2				
1				
SA	A	ID	D	SD

5. I'm not into tattoos.

Group 1				
5				
4				
3				
2				
1				
SA	A	ID	D	SD

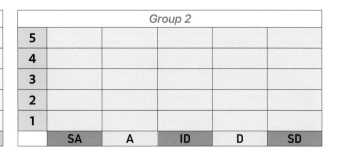

Group 2				
5				
4				
3				
2				
1				
SA	A	ID	D	SD

REPORT

Write the results of your survey. Explain the differences and similarities of fashion opinions between two groups.

For example:
- *Students in Group 1 wear designer clothes more often than students in Group 2. For example, four students in Group 1 usually wear designer clothes, but only two students in Group 2 wear designer clothes.*
- *Students in Group 2 like loose jeans more than students in Group 1. For example, seven students in Group 2 like wearing loose jeans, but only three students in Group 1 like wearing them.*

PRESENTATION

Take turns explaining the results of your survey to your classmates using the column charts in the previous page.

MODULE 3

Food

GOALS:

 Can you scan for information about food from different countries?

 Can you describe your eating habits?

 Can you understand a restaurant review?

 Can you find out about the eating habits of students?

Can you read and understand restaurant menus and restaurant reviews?

Can you write a restaurant review?

Can you understand vocabulary related to food?

UNIT 6

MATCH

Write the name of the countries in the correct space under each country's flag. Try to match countries **1-5** with food **a-e** below. Write the letter of the dish in the correct box above the flag.

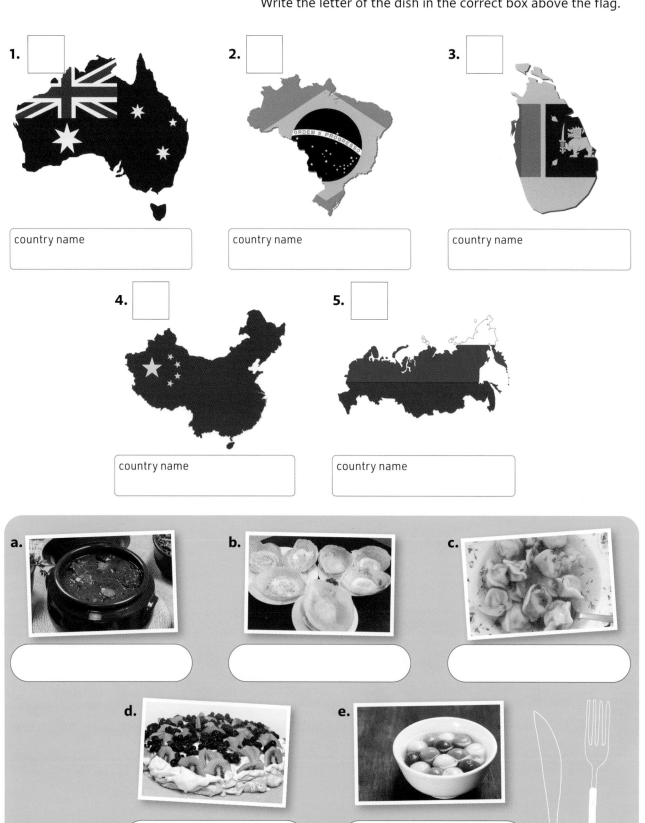

1. [ ]

country name

2. [ ]

country name

3. [ ]

country name

4. [ ]

country name

5. [ ]

country name

a.

b.

c.

d.

e.

SCAN

International food

 DL 12   CD 12

A *Scanning for information:* In 4 minutes, scan the texts below to find the key information. Check your answers on the previous page.

B Read the texts again and write the name of each dish under the correct food picture on the previous page.

1. Pavlova is my favorite dessert. It is very popular in New Zealand and Australia. It is made from meringue with fruit and fresh cream on top. We often use strawberries and kiwi fruit. We bake it in the oven, so the outside is crunchy. I usually have it in the summer, especially at Christmas. Christmas in New Zealand is in the summer.

This stew of black beans, sausages and pork is called feijoada. I like to eat it with rice. I hardly ever cook it at home because it takes a long time to make. I often go out to a restaurant to eat it. People eat this dish everywhere in Brazil, but they usually eat it on Wednesdays and Saturdays, rarely on any other days. **2.**

3.  These pancakes are called hoppers in Sri Lanka. They are shaped like bowls. I always eat them for breakfast. They have an egg at the bottom, and I usually fill them with spicy curry and vegetables. I love sweet hoppers, too. They are served with honey or coconut syrup. Delicious!

Tangyuan is a dessert that we usually eat at the Dongzhi midwinter festival (around December 22) and on the last day of the Chinese New Year (the Lantern Festival). This dish is made with colorful, sticky rice balls. It is served in a bowl with sweet ginger syrup. I always eat it at home with my family. **4.**

5.  This is a photo of a dish called pelmeni that my mother often cooks at home. These boiled Russian dumplings are filled with minced beef or pork, or a mixture of both. The dumplings in the picture are beef because I never eat pork. I'm allergic to it. It is usually served with smetana which is similar to sour cream.

C In pairs, discuss which of these dishes look the most delicious.

FOCUS

A *Describing food:* Match phrases **1-8** with pictures **a**-**h** below.

1. boiled food · · · · · · · · · · · · · · · · · · · ☐

2. deep fried food · · · · · · · · · · · · · · · · ☐

3. healthy food · · · · · · · · · · · · · · · · · · ☐

4. sour fruit · ☐

5. fast food · ☐

6. sweet desserts · · · · · · · · · · · · · · · · ☐

7. spicy food · ☐

8. fresh fish · ☐

B *Frequency:* Write a number from **1-7** in the boxes below showing the level of frequency.

I usually eat... ☐   I often eat... ☐

I rarely eat... ☐   I never eat... ☐

I sometimes eat... ☐   I always eat... ☐

I hardly eat... ☐

1   **100%**
2
⋮
7   **0%**

C *Let's talk:* In pairs, discuss your eating habits using the phrases from **A** and **B**. Try to give reasons.

For example:

A: What food do you **often** eat?
B: I **often** eat fast food.
A: Me too. I **always** eat fast food because I have no money.

LISTEN

 DL 13 · CD 13

A Listen to a restaurant blog. Write the writer's name in the box under her picture. Then put a check mark in the correct circles.

CITY   RESTAURANTS   DAYS

Name:

 DL 14 · CD 14

B Now listen to the second part of the blog and complete the text below.

I love the _____ food.

They have a lot of _____ to choose from. I usually order poppadoms
with a dip as a _____. They are thin, crispy crackers that are round
shaped.

Then, for a main course, I always order a mild _____ with naan bread.
There are many types to choose from. You can have chicken, _____,
or vegetarian with _____. I usually order chicken, it's
my _____. With my main course, I like to order a mango
lassi _____ because it's refreshing. It's made from yogurt and
goes really well with _____ food.

Finally, for _____, I often have a coffee ice cream. It's so delicious.

C Now listen to the whole blog and complete her order at the restaurant below.

Sultan's Palace

*10% discount *closed Tuesdays

Starter
　　　　Poppadoms

Main Course

Dessert

Drink

D 💬💬 Give your opinion!

1. I never eat spicy food.

Agree: _____　　Disagree: _____

Why? _____

2. I often eat fresh vegetables.

Agree: _____　　Disagree: _____

Why? _____

3. Which do you prefer, meat or fish dishes?

Answer: _____

Why? _____

4. What restaurants do you recommend?

Answer: _____

Why? _____

COMMUNICATE

What are the eating habits of students?

A Write your answers to the questions in the "Your answer" column. Then, ask a classmate and write their answers in the "Partner's answer" column. Finally, in groups, discuss what you think is the most popular answer for university students and write your group's guess in the "Most popular answer" column.

Question	Your Answer	Partner's Answer	Most popular answer (Group's guess)
1. What dessert do you often eat?			
2. What vegetable do you hardly ever eat?			
3. What do you like to drink when you are thirsty?			
4. What do people often eat in the summer?			
5. What food do you think tastes sour?			
6. What dish do you think is spicy?			
7. What food is Osaka famous for?			
8. What dish are you good at cooking?			
9. What do you usually have for breakfast?			
10. What dish do you think is healthy?			

B Think of two more questions that you would like to ask about food and write them in the table below. Write your answers and then ask your classmate the questions to complete the table.

Question	Your Answer	Partner's Answer
11.		
12.		

UNIT 7

READ
Restaurant menus and reviews

A *Brainstorm:* What is the name of your favorite restaurant? Think of reasons why you like it.

For example: My favorite restaurant is called … I like it because ….

B *Pre-reading:* Read the menu below and try to guess the missing words.

GREAT FOOD, GREAT SERVICE, GREAT TIMES

Franco's Italian Restaurant

(10% discount for students)

Open for breakfast,
l_____ & dinner
Last orders 10:00 p.m.
Closed on Wednesdays

L_____ MENU

Starters   All $5
Hot
•*Minestrone soup* - v_____ soup
•*Calamari* - deep-f_____ squid
Cold
•*Caesar salad*
  - lettuce, olive oil, soft-boiled egg, black
    olives, Parmesan cheese
•*Caprese salad*
  - fresh mozzarella cheese, tomatoes, sweet
    basil, olive oil

Side Items   All $4
•*F_____ potatoes*
•*Freshly b _____ Italian bread*
•*Garlic rice*
•*Boiled v_____*

Drinks   All $3
Hot
•*f_____ orange juice*   •*cola*
•*lemonade*   •*mineral water*
•*coffee*   •*tea*
Cold
•*coffee*   •*tea*

Main Courses   All $10
•FRANCO'S FAMOUS PIZZA
  Margherita - mozzarella cheese, tomatoes
  Seafood - clams, squid, shrimp, crab
  Pepperoni - s_____ Italian sausage

•FRANCO'S F_____ PASTA
  Carbonara - egg, bacon, Parmesan cheese
  Peperoncino - s_____ chili and garlic
                in olive oil
  Lasagna - b_____ pasta with minced
            beef in tomato
                     s_____

D_____   All $4
•*Tiramisu* - coffee-flavored Italian d_____
•*Italian chocolate cake*
•*Panna cotta* - cream pudding with raspberry
                 s_____
•*Assorted Italian ice cream*

C Check the hints in the box below (each word is used twice) and complete the menu. Then decide what
you would like to eat and drink for under $25.

| baked | dessert(s) | fresh | fried | lunch | sauce | spicy | vegetable(s) |

DL 16   CD 16

D Read Paul's review of Franco's restaurant. Complete the menu below showing the food that Paul usually orders from Franco's restaurant, as well as details of Franco's restaurant.

PAUL'S FOOD BLOG

Hello everyone. Today I'm reviewing my favorite Italian restaurant: Franco's. I'm a regular customer at Franco's, and I often go there with my wife and kids. It is a fantastic restaurant because the meals are great! The waiters are really friendly and helpful, and the owner, Franco, always makes you feel very welcome.

The food here is the best! I love their healthy salads. I especially like the Caesar salad. I always have that for starter. The soft-boiled egg is delicious. Their deep-fried calamari tastes really good too, but it is a little salty. And the vegetables in the minestrone soup are fresh and tasty. For main course, I usually have the beef lasagna. The tomato sauce is great but be careful, it's freshly baked in the oven, so it is really hot. So I have that with a cold drink, usually ice water. For people who are into spicy dishes, I recommend the peperoncino pasta. If I'm still hungry, I usually have the panna cotta for dessert. The raspberry sauce is amazing. My kids always have the Italian ice cream. They love it.

Franco's is a popular restaurant, but it's not so expensive, especially the lunch menu. There is a 10% discount for students, so it's quite cheap. It's really busy on Saturdays and Sundays but not so much during the week. It's a good idea to make a reservation on weekends. They are closed on Wednesdays. I'm definitely going to Franco's again soon! It's my birthday in three weeks and Franco's is the place I want to enjoy it.

PAUL'S RATING ★ ★ ★ ★ ★

MENU

Closed: _____

Students: _____ discount.

Starter: _____

Main course:

_____

Drink: _____

Dessert: _____

Franco's

A *Word check:* Complete this review of a restaurant. Use words from the vocabulary box below to help you.

My favorite place to eat out is called "Happy Chef." It's a Western-style restaurant near my university. It's a fantastic restaurant because the food is amazing and the _____ is great.

The food is awesome! I often eat their Hamburg steak. It comes with rice or _____ potatoes. The set _____ is served with a _____ side salad. I also like the desserts at Happy Chef. I usually eat apple pie. The fruit tastes nice and _____ and the _____ cream is delicious.

I usually go to this restaurant on weekdays and it's open until 10 o'clock in the evening. It is _____ on weekends because lots of families go there. I especially like the lunch menu because it is quite _____. For 1,000 yen you can have three _____. You get a starter, a main course and a dessert. Lunch is from 11:00 a.m. to 2:30 p.m. The restaurant is _____ every Tuesday.

fried   busy   menu   sweet   healthy   service   closed   cheap   courses   fresh

B *Writing skill:* Descriptive paragraph writing

▶ First, write a main idea about the topic (topic sentence). Then, write details about it (supporting details).

For example: *(Topic sentence) The food is great.*
             (Supporting details) The fried potatoes are really tasty.

C *Let's Practice:* Complete your answers to the questions below.

1. What's the name of your favorite restaurant? Why do you like it?

   My favorite restaurant is _____. I like it because _____

   _____.

2. How is the food? Give examples.

   Their food is _____. I love their _____.

   I also like _____.

3. When do you go there? Is it busy? Is it expensive?

   I usually go there _____. During the week, _____

   _____. The prices are _____.

D *Task:* Write a review of your favorite restaurant. Structure your writing into 3 short paragraphs.

For example:
Paragraph 1: Describe the restaurant and give 1 or 2 reasons why you like it.

Paragraph 2: Write about the food and your favorite meals/drinks.

Paragraph 3: When do you go there? Is it busy? Is it expensive?

Use the space below to plan your writing.

My Favorite Restaurant

VOCABULARY

DL 17   CD 17

Adjectives		hungry A1		hardly A2 ever A2		fast food A2	
bitter B1		open A1		never A1		fish A1	
boiled A2		popular A2		often A1		fruit A1	
busy A1		salty B2		rarely B1		lunch A1	
careful A1		sour B1		sometimes B1		meal A1	
cheap A2		spicy B1		usually A1		meat A1	
closed A1		sweet A1		**Nouns**		salad B1	
delicious A1		tasty B1		breakfast A1		service B1	
expensive A1		thirsty A2		dessert A2		vegetable A1	
fresh A2		unhealthy A2		diet A2		**Verbs**	
fried A2		**Adverbs (Frequency)**		dinner A1		cook A1	
healthy A1		always A1		dish A1		taste B1	

A Match each definition with the words on the right.

1. A meal you eat in the evening: _____   a. vegetables
2. Plants that you can eat: _____   b. dinner
3. When you want something to drink: _____   c. bitter
4. having a sharp and often unpleasant taste: _____   d. thirsty

B Write a word with the opposite meaning to the words below.

1. sweet ⟷ _____

2. expensive ⟷ _____

3. never ⟷ _____

4. healthy ⟷ _____

C Choose the words from the box that best complete the questions. Answer the questions.

> vegetables   fried   sour   time   cooking

1. Do you often eat deep [_____] food?   A: _____

2. Do you like [_____] fruit?   A: _____

3. What [_____] do you never eat?   A: _____

4. What are you good at [_____] ?   A: _____

5. What [_____] do you usually eat dinner?   A: _____

D *Crossword:* Complete the crossword using the hints below.

Across

2. My diet is quite _____ . I rarely eat fast food.

3. I don't like grapefruit. It is really _____ .

7.

8. I like milk chocolate, but I think dark chocolate is too _____ .

9.

12. I _____ have coffee at breakfast. I drink it every morning.

14. I can't _____ at all. I can't even boil an egg!

15.

16.

17. The food at that new restaurant _____ really bad. Don't go there.

Down

1. I _____ eat peanuts. I'm allergic to them.

2.

4. In Japan, _____ chicken is popular at Christmas.

5.

6.

8. I don't eat _____ . I'm so busy in the morning.

10.

11. _____ soda drinks are bad for your health.

13.

16.

Adverbs of frequency

Yes/No questions about eating habits

Adverbs of frequency		Yes/No questions	
100%	always	Do you usually drink coffee in the morning?	No, I don't. I hardly ever drink coffee.
	usually		
		Do you cook dinner at home?	Yes, I do. I usually cook Chinese food.
	often		
		Does your brother often eat out with friends?	Yes, he does. He always goes out for ramen noodles.
	sometimes		
	rarely	Does your mother eat fast food?	No, she doesn't. She never eats unhealthy food.
	hardly ever		
0%	never	Do your friends usually eat chocolate at lunchtime?	Yes, they do. They often buy chocolate at the convenience store.

A Put the questions in the correct order and answer them.

1. [friends / out / eat / your / with / you / do]?

Q._____

A._____

2. [lunch / do / what / usually / for / eat / you]?

Q._____

A._____

3. [you / what / food / kind / do / of / eat / often]?

Q._____

A._____

B Complete the sentences about your eating habits using adverbs of frequency from the box below.

always   usually   often   sometimes   rarely   hardly ever   never

1. I _____ drink coffee in the morning.   2. I _____ drink fresh fruit juice.

3. I _____ go out to eat on weekends.   4. I _____ eat fast food.

5. I _____ cook in the evening.   6. I _____ eat spicy food.

MODULE 3 SELF-CHECK

Write a score (1-5)* in the boxes below to show how well you can do each part of the module. If you can't do any part well, go back to the page and practice again.

* 1 : Not at all   **2 :** A little   **3 :** OK   **4 :** Well   **5 :** Very well

UNIT 6

SCAN

I can scan for information about food from different countries (p.45). ⋯⋯⋯⋯⋯⋯

FOCUS

I can discribe my eating habits (p.46). ⋯⋯⋯⋯⋯⋯⋯⋯⋯⋯⋯⋯⋯⋯⋯⋯

LISTEN

I can understand a restaurant review (p.47-48). ⋯⋯⋯⋯⋯⋯⋯⋯⋯⋯⋯⋯

COMMUNICATE

I can ask and answer questions about eating habits (p.49). ⋯⋯⋯⋯⋯⋯

UNIT 7

READ

I can read and understand restaurant menus and restaurant reviews (p.50-51). ⋯⋯⋯

WRITE

I can write a restaurant review (p.52-53). ⋯⋯⋯⋯⋯⋯⋯⋯⋯⋯⋯⋯⋯⋯

VOCABULARY

I can understand vocabulary related to food (p.54-55). ⋯⋯⋯⋯⋯⋯⋯⋯⋯

MODULE 4

Lifestyles

GOALS:

 Can you scan for information about people's lifestyles ?

 Can you describe your health and lifestyle?

 Can you understand a lifestyle podcast?

 Can you find out about the lifestyle differences of your classmates?

Can you read and understand people's work lifestyles?

Can you write about your lifestyle?

Can you understand vocabulary related to lifestyle?

UNIT 8

MATCH / SCAN / FOCUS / LISTEN / COMMUNICATE

MATCH

Look at pictures **1-5**. Try to guess which lifestyle matches person **a-e** below. Write the letter of the person in the boxes below.

1.

2.

3.

4.

5.

a.

b.

c.

d.

e.

SCAN

Lifestyles

DL 18 CD 18

A *Scanning for information:* <u>In 4 minutes</u>, scan the texts below to find the key information. Check your answers on the previous page.

B Read the texts again and write the name of each person's job in the correct space on the previous page.

1.

My name is Ken. I'm retired now, and I'm really relaxed! I really like going hiking in the mountains with my wife. I go to bed early and always get enough sleep. I eat a lot of fresh vegetables and often have salad for lunch. I love eating desserts. I eat them almost every day!

2.

I'm Maya. I work really hard, and I have a lot of stress. I smoke a lot, and I always drink wine in the evening. I like playing tennis, but I can't play very often because I'm always busy at work. I'm a lawyer, so I work long hours and don't get enough sleep.

3.

I'm James, and I'm a university student. My major is Business. I work part-time as a waiter at a coffee shop. I love coffee, and I usually drink two or three cups a day. I often stay up late studying, so I don't have much free time in the morning. I never eat breakfast. I don't often go to the gym, but I go snowboarding every winter.

4.

My name is Kyle. I'm not interested in sports, and I don't do any exercise. I enjoy relaxing at home and watching TV. I usually eat junk food in the evening. I'm putting on weight now. I'm an office worker, so I spend most of the day sitting down. I'm worried about my health.

5.

I'm Nina. I love doing exercise. I go jogging almost every evening and go to the gym three times a week. I love meat, and my favorite food is steak. I eat meat every day. I also like eating fruit. I usually eat bananas after exercise. I am a high school PE teacher, so I need to keep fit.

C In pairs, discuss which person from above is similar to your lifestyle. Describe your lifestyle to your classmate. Think about diet, exercise and sleep.

FOCUS

A *Lifestyle:* Match phrases **1-8** with pictures **a-h** below.

1. fruit lover · · · · · · · · · · · · · · · · · · · ☐

2. exercise nut · · · · · · · · · · · · · · · · · ☐

3. chocoholic · · · · · · · · · · · · · · · · · ☐

4. couch potato · · · · · · · · · · · · · · · ☐

5. stress head · ☐

6. game addict · · · · · · · · · · · · · · · · · · ☐

7. night owl · ☐

8. bookworm · · · · · · · · · · · · · · · · · · · ☐

a.

b.

c.

d.

e.

f.

g.

h.

B Describe your lifestyle using the frequency expressions and examples below.

frequency expressions	examples
I always... / I usually... / I often....	stay up late / play games online
I sometimes... / I rarely...	get stressed / read books.
I hardly ever... / I never...	eat chocolate / exercise
	go to bed early / eat fruit

C 💬💬 *Let's talk:* Is your lifestyle similar to any of the pictures in part **A**? Practice describing your lifestyle.

For example:

A: I usually eat chocolate in the evening. I think I'm a chocoholic.
B: Really? I hardly ever eat chocolate.
A: I'm not a couch potato. I usually go jogging in the evening.
B: That's good. Jogging is good exercise.

LISTEN

A lifestyle podcast

 DL 19 ◎ CD 19

A Listen to the first part of the podcast. Write the speaker's name in the box under his picture. Then put a check mark in the correct circles.

COUNTRY

HOW MANY MARATHONS?

WHICH CITIES?

PARIS
SYDNEY
TOKYO

LONDON
NEW YORK
TOKYO

Name:

B Now listen to the rest of the podcast and complete the text below.

 DL 20 ◎ CD 20

(Presenter: I see so to prepare for a marathon, how often do you go running?)

Well, my training begins about four _____ before a marathon. I start by running six days a

week but because I work for a Bank during the week, I do my long runs at the _____ .

So on Sundays, I start running _____ kilometers and then I run further each week.

(Presenter: I see, and what about your diet for a marathon? How much protein do you eat?)

Well, I need to make sure I get enough _____ because my training increases each week.

So I have _____ meals a day with lots of protein snacks. I can't drink any soda drinks or eat

junk food. I need a balanced diet of fruit, _____ and protein: white meat, fish and eggs.

I also need carbohydrates: bread, rice, potatoes, _____ .

C Now listen to the whole of the podcast and complete the details below about the runner's exercise, diet, and rest / sleep.

George: Marathon runner

Exercise	Diet	Rest / Sleep

Exercise

Begins 4 months before a marathon

Run _____ a week

Run _____ on Sundays and then further each week

Diet

Have 3 meals a day with lots of _____

Don't drink _____ and eat _____

Need a balanced diet of _____ and protein: _____

Also need _____: bread, rice, potatoes, pasta

Rest / Sleep

Rest _____

Try to sleep _____ every night

D 💬💬 Give your opinion!

1. Jogging is the best way to keep fit.

Agree: _____   Disagree: _____

Why? _____

2. I would like to run a marathon.

Agree: _____   Disagree: _____

Why? _____

3. White rice is healthy.

Agree: _____   Disagree: _____

Why? _____

4. Getting enough sleep helps to prevent injuries.

Agree: _____   Disagree: _____

Why? _____

COMMUNICATE   How healthy is your lifestyle?

A First, write your answers to the questions in "Your Answer." Check your lifestyle score (1-4) using the table below.

B Next, interview 2 classmates and write their answers in the "Partner 1" and "Partner 2" columns. Check your partners' lifestyle scores.

Question (Score)	You	Partner 1	Partner 2
1 How many nights a week don't you get enough sleep? (**A**=every night **B**=4 or 5 nights **C**=2 or 3 nights **D**=I usually get enough sleep)			
2 How often do you exercise? (**A**=hardly ever **B**=a few times a month **C**=once or twice a week **D**=almost every day)			
3 How many times a year do you get a cold? (**A**=I never get colds **B**=once **C**=2 or 3 times **D**=4 times or more)			
4 How much junk food do you eat? (**A**=hardly any **B**=not so much **C**=quite a lot **D**=a lot)			
5 How much time do you spend online or playing video games? (**A**=hardly any **B**=1 or 2 hours a day **C**=3 or 4 hours a day **D**=more than 5 hours a day)			
6 How often do you clean your teeth? (**A**=not every day **B**=once a day **C**=twice a day **D**=3 times a day or more)			
7 How many sugary soda drinks do you drink? (**A**=hardly any **B**=1 or 2 a week **C**=almost every day **D**=1 or more a day)			
8 How many portions of fruit and vegetables do you eat a day? (**A**=none **B**=1 or 2 **C**=3-5 **D**=6 or more)			
9 How often do you skip breakfast? (**A**=every day **B**=2 or 3 times a week **C**=3 or 4 times a month **D**=never)			
10 How much chocolate or sweet food do you eat? (**A**=a lot **B**=quite a lot **C**=not so much **D**=hardly any)			
TOTAL			

Scores

1 A=1 B=2 C=3 D=4
2 A=1 B=2 C=3 D=4
3 A=4 B=3 C=2 D=1
4 A=4 B=3 C=2 D=1
5 A=4 B=3 C=2 D=1
6 A=1 B=2 C=3 D=4
7 A=4 B=3 C=2 D=1
8 A=1 B=2 C=3 D=4
9 A=1 B=2 C=3 D=4
10 A=1 B=2 C=3 D=4

Score Ratings

32-40	Congratulations! You have a very healthy lifestyle. Keep it up!
23-31	Don't worry! You are pretty healthy, but you should try to improve some things.
14-22	You are not so healthy. You need to change your lifestyle!

READ
Work lifestyle

A *Brainstorm:* What is the best way to have a healthy lifestyle?

For example: Eating a balanced diet, exercising regularly, getting enough sleep.

B *Pre-reading:* Maya is a lawyer. Look at the pictures below to see how her job affects her lifestyle in terms of diet, exercise and sleep. First, write the correct number for the each pictures in the circles next to the phrases on the left side. Then, match the connected phrases below.

1 In the morning, I have a cup of coffee on the way to work.

I like playing tennis,

On Sundays, I sleep late and spend a lot of time on my phone.

I sometimes get headaches at work,

I usually order a pizza

I smoke and drink wine in the evening to relax,

Two or three times a week, I stay up late working,

when I don't get enough rest or get enough sleep.

which is not so good for my health.

I don't usually have time to eat breakfast.

but I haven't played recently because I rarely have the time.

so I can't sleep well.

I'm usually too tired to play tennis or exercise after a busy week.

or buy some junk food on my way home.

DL 22   CD 22

C Read about Maya's lifestyle as a busy lawyer. Complete the details below about her diet, exercise and sleep. List the negative (-) and positive (+) examples of her lifestyle.

⌲ *How healthy is your liferstyle?*

My name is Maya. I'm a lawyer at a major law firm in London, UK. I like my job but it's very stressful. I work long hours, so I don't get much free time. Recently, I've been very busy, and I don't think I have a healthy lifestyle now.

In the morning, I have a cup of coffee on the way to work. I don't usually have time to eat breakfast. I try to have a healthy lunch, so I have a fresh salad sandwich or something like that every day. I often work late, so I hardly ever have time to cook when I get home. I usually order a pizza or buy some junk food on my way home. I smoke and drink wine in the evening to relax, which is not so good for my health.

I like playing tennis, but I haven't played recently because I rarely have the time. One positive thing is that I walk a lot because I have to travel into the city every day to meet my clients. On Sundays, I sleep late and spend a lot of time on my phone. I'm usually too tired to play tennis or exercise after a busy week.

I try to sleep at least seven hours a night which gives me enough rest to work the next day. Two or three times a week, I stay up late working, so I can't sleep well. I sometimes get headaches at work, when I don't get enough rest or get enough sleep. I think I should have a healthier lifestyle.

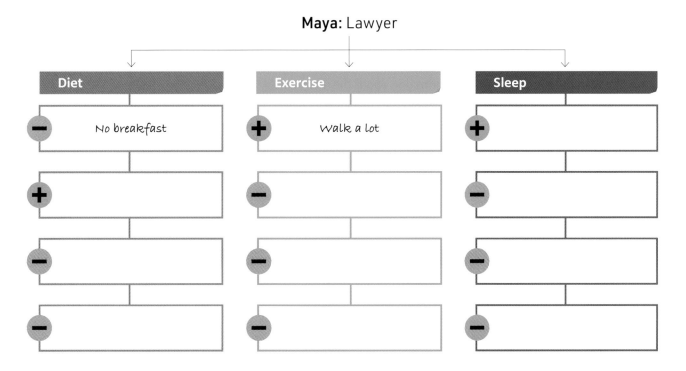

Maya: Lawyer

Diet	Exercise	Sleep
(-) No breakfast	(+) Walk a lot	(+)
(+)	(-)	(-)
(-)	(-)	(-)
(-)	(-)	(-)

D In pairs, discuss how your lifestyle is similar or different to Maya.

WRITE

A *Word check:* Complete James's lifestyle below about his diet, exercise and sleep. Use words from the vocabulary box below to help you.

I have a pretty unhealthy diet. I'm a university student and I work part-time as a _____ so I don't have the time or _____ to cook healthy food. I never eat breakfast, I just have a coffee in the _____. For lunch and dinner I usually eat fast food such as ramen or a burrito from a convenience store. Fast food is _____ but it's tasty.

I don't exercise much because I have to study and I'm _____ with my part-time job. I work four days a week at a coffee shop. I don't play _____ or go to the gym but during the holidays I like to exercise. I have more _____ then. In the winter I go snowboarding, and in _____ I go surfing. It's a lot of fun!

I don't sleep much during the week. After work, I stay up late _____ or I go online so I'm always tired in the morning. Sometimes I'm late for my first period class! At the weekends, I sleep more because I have no _____. I'm not a morning person so I usually sleep in on Saturdays and Sundays.

cheap	sports	waiter	morning	free time
classes	busy	summer	studying	money

B *Writing skill:* Descriptive paragraph writing

- ● Writing main ideas with supporting examples
  - For example: *(Main idea) I don't have a healthy diet.*
- ● Supporting examples provide information about the main idea.
  - For example: *(Supporting examples) I always eat cup ramen for dinner.*

C *Let's Practice:* Write a main idea followed by examples about your lifestyle. Write about the following three topics:

1. Diet

I _____

2. Exercise

I _____

3. Sleep

I _____

D *Task:* Write about your lifestyle below using the examples from the previous page. Write three paragraphs about your diet, exercise and sleep.

My lifestyle

VOCABULARY

Adjectives		less ^A2^	....	jogging ^B1^	....	yoga ^B1^	....

Adjectives

balanced ^B2^ (diet)

....

fit ^A2^ ....

negative ^A2^ ....

positive ^B1^ ....

relaxed ^A2^ ....

stressed ^B1^ ....

stressful ^B1^ ....

tired ^A1^ ....

Adverbs

further ^B1^ ....

enough ^A2^ ....

least ^B1^ ....

less ^A2^ ....

more ^B1/A1^ ....

once ^A1^ ....

pretty ^A2^ ....

recently ^A2^ ....

twice ^A2^ ....

Nouns

addict ^B2^ ....

carbohydrate(s) + ...

coffee ^A1^ ....

cold ^A1^ ....

cough ^B2^ ....

dentist ^A2^ ....

exercise ^A2^ ....

jogging ^B1^ ....

headache ^A1^ ....

health ^A1^ ....

junk food ^B2^ ....

kilometer ^A2^ ....

lifestyle ^A2^ ....

marathon ^B2^ ....

medicine ^A1^ ....

protein + ...

rest ^B1^ ....

sleep ^B1^ ....

snack ^A2^ ....

stress ^B1^ ....

training ^A2^ ....

yoga ^B1^ ....

Verbs

exercise ^A1^ ....

feel ^A1^ (tired ^A1^) ....

gain ^B1^ (weight ^A2^) ....

increase ^A2^ ....

lose ^A2^ (weight ^A2^) ....

quit ^A2^ ....

relax ^A2^ ....

sleep ^A1^ ....

spend ^A1^ ....

worry ^A2^ ....

A Match each definition with the words on the right.

1. A drug that is used to treat illness: _____
2. A person who looks after your teeth: _____
3. The way that you live: _____
4. A bitter drink people often have in the morning: _____

    a. lifestyle
    b. medicine
    c. dentist
    d. coffee

B Write a word with the opposite meaning to the words below.

1. lose weight   ↔ _____

2. _____ ↔ more

3. _____ ↔ stressed

4. positive   ↔ _____

C Choose the words from the box that best complete the questions. Answer the questions.

lifestyle   much   many   often   exercise

1. How [_____] hours do you sleep at night?   A: _____

2. How [_____] junk food do you eat a week?   A: _____

3. How [_____] do you clean your teeth a day?   A: _____

4. How often do you [_____] ?   A: _____

5. How healthy is your [_____] ?   A: _____

D *Crossword:* Complete the crossword using the hints below.

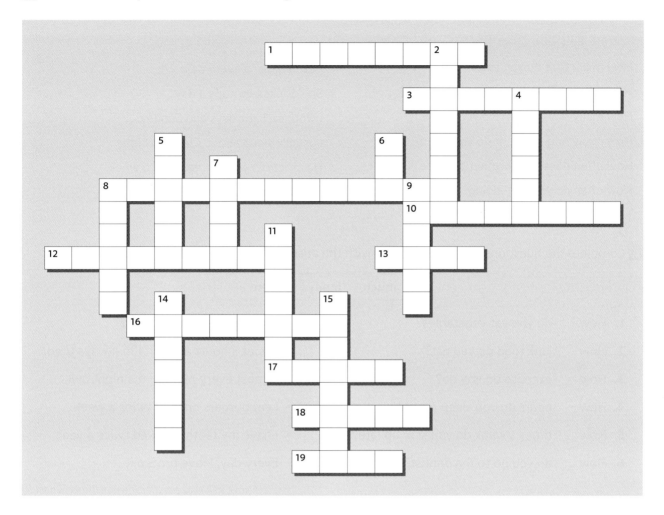

Across

1. Food is important for your health. You should eat a ____ diet

3.

8.

10.

12. How healthy is your ____ ?

13. How much ____ food do you eat?

16.

17. I brush my teeth ____ a day. Once in the morning and once at night.

18.

19. Try to take a ____ . You are working too hard.

Down

2. I often play sport and ____ at the gym.

4.
   game _____

5.
   _____ head

6. Swimming is a good way to keep ____ .

7. Don't ____ ! Try to relax.

8.

9. You need to sleep more. Five hours a night is not ____ .

11.

14.

15. I have a cold. I need to take ____ .

LANGUAGE REVIEW

Asking "How" questions and giving answers about lifestyle

"How" questions (present tense)	Giving answers
How much fruit do you eat?	I eat a banana every day.
How much coffee does your friend drink?	She drinks two cups a day.
How many days a week do you work?	I work on Saturdays and Sundays.
How many hours a night do you sleep?	I usually sleep about 7 hours a night.
How often does your brother practice yoga?	He practices yoga three times a week.
How often do you go jogging?	I go jogging four times a week.

A Complete the questions, then match them with the answers.

| much | many | often |

1. How ___ do you eat vegetables? •
2. How ___ junk food do you eat? •
3. How ___ exercise do you do? •
4. How ___ hours do you sleep a night? •
5. How ___ times a week do you stay up late? •
6. How ___ do you go to the dentist? •

• I play tennis twice a week.
• About 5 hours a night. I'm always tired.
• Almost every night. I'm a night owl.
• I eat burgers once or twice a week.
• I have my teeth checked twice a year.
• Every day. I love broccoli!

Now, ask your partner the questions in part B.

B Put the words in the correct order.

1. [exercises / twice / week / a / my friend].

   _____

2. [tennis / plays / my father / three / a / times / week].

   _____

3. [sushi / once / eat / I / week / a].

   _____

4. [rarely / sleep / more / than / hours / 6 / I / day / a].

   _____

5. [I / take / should / medicine / often / how]?

   _____

6. [often / your brother / does / fast food / eat / how]?

   _____

MODULE 4 SELF-CHECK

Write a score (1-5)* in the boxes below to show how well you can do each part of the module. If you can't do any part well, go back to the page and practice again.

* **1 :** Not at all   **2 :** A little   **3 :** OK   **4 :** Well   **5 :** Very well

UNIT 8

SCAN

I can scan for information about lifestyles (p.61). ⋯⋯⋯⋯⋯⋯⋯⋯⋯⋯⋯

FOCUS

I can describe my lifestyle using adverbs of frequency (p.62). ⋯⋯⋯⋯⋯

LISTEN

I can understand a lifestyle podcast about diet, exercise and sleep (p.63-64). ⋯⋯⋯⋯

COMMUNICATE

I can talk about my health and lifestyle (p.65). ⋯⋯⋯⋯⋯⋯⋯⋯⋯⋯

UNIT 9

READ

I can read someone's description of their diet, exercise and sleep (p.66-67). ⋯⋯⋯⋯⋯

WRITE

I can write about my diet, exercise and sleep (p.68-69). ⋯⋯⋯⋯⋯⋯⋯

VOCABULARY

I can understand vocabulary related to lifestyle (p.70-71). ⋯⋯⋯⋯⋯⋯

PROJECT C

What are the eating habits of your classmates?

You are going to survey 10 classmates to find out their eating habits. Ask 10 classmates the questions below and note their answers in the tables.

1. What do you usually eat for breakfast?

	Rice	Bread	Miso soup	Fruit	Other
Number					
%					

2. What do you usually drink in the morning?

	Coffee	Tea	Orange juice	Soda	Other
Number					
%					

3. What is your favorite dessert?

	Ice cream	Chocolate cake	Cheesecake	Strawberry shortcake	Other
Number					
%					

4. What international food do you often eat?

	Chinese	Italian	American	Indian	Other
Number					
%					

5. What restaurant do you often go to?*

					Other
Number					
%					

6. What is your favorite convenience store?*

				Other
Number				
%				

*Write the names of the most popular answers in the pink boxes.

RESULTS

Column Charts

Based on the numbers in the previous page, complete the column charts for each question below.

1. What do you usually eat for breakfast?

10					
9					
8					
7					
6					
5					
4					
3					
2					
1					
	Rice	Bread	Miso soup	Fruit	Other

2. What do you usually drink in the morning?

10					
9					
8					
7					
6					
5					
4					
3					
2					
1					
	Coffee	Tea	Orange juice	Soda	Other

3. What is your favorite dessert?

10					
9					
8					
7					
6					
5					
4					
3					
2					
1					
	Ice cream	Chocolate cake	Cheese cake	Strawberry shortcake	Other

4. What international food do you often eat?

10					
9					
8					
7					
6					
5					
4					
3					
2					
1					
	Chinese	Italian	American	Indian	Other

5. What restaurant do you often go to?

10					
9					
8					
7					
6					
5					
4					
3					
2					
1					
					Other

6. What is your favorite convenience store?

10					
9					
8					
7					
6					
5					
4					
3					
2					
1					
					Other

REPORT

Write the results of your survey and suggest reasons.

For example: *In my group, 80% of students said they drink tea in the morning. I think tea is popular because it's healthy.*

PRESENTATION

Take turns explaining the results of your survey to your classmates using the column charts in the previous page.

PROJECT D

Who has the healthier lifestyle?

Choose two different groups. Then ask 10 students (5 from each group) about the following lifestyle topics: food, drink, exercise, sleep and stress. Note their answers (**A, B, C** or **D**), their scores (**1, 2, 3** or **4**) and the total in the tables.

1. Food: How much junk food or unhealthy food do you eat?

A=a lot, I love it! **B**=quite a lot **C**=not so much **D**=hardly any, I don't like it! (**A**=1, **B**=2, **C**=3, **D**=4)

		Student 1	Student 2	Student 3	Student 4	Student 5	Total
Group 1	Answer						
	Score						/20
Group 2	Answer						
	Score						/20

2. Drink: How often do you drink soda or sugary drinks?

A=every day **B**=2 or 3 times a week **C**=3 or 4 times a month **D**=hardly ever (**A**=1, **B**=2, **C**=3, **D**=4)

		Student 1	Student 2	Student 3	Student 4	Student 5	Total
Group 1	Answer						
	Score						/20
Group 2	Answer						
	Score						/20

3. Exercise: How often do you play sports or go to the gym?

A=every day **B**=once or twice a week **C**=once or twice a month **D**=hardly ever (**A**=4, **B**=3, **C**=2, **D**=1)

		Student 1	Student 2	Student 3	Student 4	Student 5	Total
Group 1	Answer						
	Score						/20
Group 2	Answer						
	Score						/20

4. Sleep: How many hours a night do you usually sleep?

A=about 8 hours **B**=6-7 hours **C**=about 5 hours **D**=less than 5 hours (**A**=4, **B**=3, **C**=2, **D**=1)

		Student 1	Student 2	Student 3	Student 4	Student 5	Total
Group 1	Answer						
	Score						/20
Group 2	Answer						
	Score						/20

5. Stress: How much stress do you have?

A=a lot **B**=quite a lot **C**=not a lot **D**=no stress (**A**=1, **B**=2, **C**=3, **D**=4)

		Student 1	Student 2	Student 3	Student 4	Student 5	Total
Group 1	Answer						
	Score						/20
Group 2	Answer						
	Score						/20

RESULTS

Spider charts

Based on the data in the previous page, complete the spider charts below.

For example:

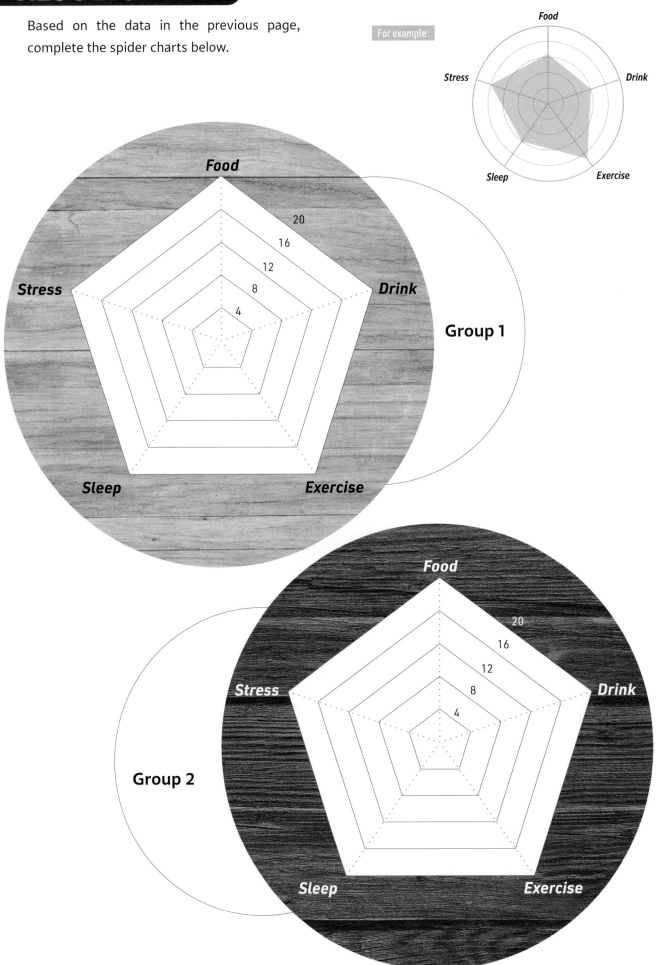

Group 1

Group 2

REPORT

Write the results of your survey

1. Report the results from the previous page. Explain any differences between the lifestyles of Group 1 and Group 2.
2. Give advice for any lifestyle changes.

For example:
- *Group 1 drink more sugary drinks than Group 2. For example, five Group 1 students drink sugary drinks every day but only one Group 2 student drinks sugary drinks. I think Group 1 should drink tea because it is healthier.*

PRESENTATION

Take turns explaining the results of your survey using the spider charts in the previous page.

MODULE 5

Travel

GOALS:

 Can you scan for information about famous places?

 Can you describe your past vacations or trips?

 Can you understand a travel blog?

 Can you answer questions about travel?

Can you read and understand postcards and vacation reviews?

Can you write about a trip you had?

Can you understand vocabulary related to travel?

MATCH / SCAN / FOCUS / LISTEN / COMMUNICATE

MATCH

Look at pictures **1-6**. Try to guess which famous sightseeing places match countries **a-f** below.

SCAN

Famous places

DL 24 · CD 24

A *Scanning for information:* In 4 minutes, scan the texts below to find the key information. Check your answers on the previous page.

B Read the texts again and write the name of the famous places in the correct space on the previous page.

1.

I had a great vacation in France. I did so much sightseeing in Paris. I visited lots of famous museums and ate some amazing food. I climbed to the top of the Eiffel tower. The view was amazing. I also went to Notre Dame, the famous cathedral in the center of Paris. I bought my parents some wine as a souvenir.

Last year, I visited India for the first time. It is an incredible country, but the weather was so hot and humid. The food was also very hot. I love spicy curry, so I really enjoyed the food. The best place I visited was the Taj Mahal. It is a UNESCO World Heritage Site and one of the most beautiful buildings in the world.

2.

3.

I really wanted to go to Machu Picchu, so I flew to Peru last December. It rained quite a lot, and it was cloudy at the top of the mountain. I took a train to Machu Picchu and then went trekking along the Inca Trail. The scenery was fantastic. I bought alpaca wool hats and scarves for my friends.

My best vacation ever was when I went to Angkor Wat. Angkor Wat is a huge temple near the town of Siem Reap in Cambodia. I stayed in a hotel with a large pool. The staff at the hotel were great, and the people I met were so friendly. I had a really good tour guide who showed me around, and we even went to a jungle temple. Later, I went on a cycling tour of the local villages.

4.

5.

During the spring holiday, I went on a group tour to Egypt. First, we took a sightseeing bus to Luxor, and then we returned to Cairo. From Cairo we visited the Pyramids of Giza. We rode on a camel in the desert before returning to the hotel. The weather was very hot during the day, but it was quite cool at night.

6.

I studied abroad in Germany for three months. I stayed with a homestay family in Munich. At the weekend, we often went to the park for a picnic and ate German sausages. I also went on a river cruise. The most beautiful place I visited was Neuschwanstein Castle. It looks like the Sleeping Beauty Castle. I took a lot of photographs and sent my friends postcards of the view.

C In pairs, describe your favorite trip to your classmate.
Where did you go? Who did you go with? What did you do?

Describing past vacations

A *Vacations:* Match phrases **1-8** with pictures **a-h** below.

1. We ate lobster. ·················· [ ]

2. The weather was nice and sunny ··· [ ]

3. The flight was long and tiring. ····· [ ]

4. I went surfing. ················ [ ]

5. I bought koala toys. ············ [ ]

6. We stayed in really nice hotel. ····· [ ]

7. The scenery was amazing! ········ [ ]

8. We saw the Sydney Opera House. ·· [ ]

a.
b.
c.
d.

e.
f.
g.
h.

B *Vacation questions:* Match the questions below with phrases **1-8** as the answers.

How was the weather? ( )

What did you do? ( )

What souvenirs did you buy? ( )

How was the journey? ( )

Where did you stay? ( )

What did you eat? ( )

What did you see there? ( )

How was the scenery? ( )

C 💬💬 *Let's talk:* In pairs, talk about trips you enjoyed in Japan or abroad. First, try the example below then talk about your own experiences.

For example:

A: I enjoyed my trip to Australia.

B: Cool! How was the weather? ➜ A: The weather was nice and sunny.

B: How was the journey? ➜ A: The flight was long and tiring.

B: Where did you stay? ➜ A: We stayed in a really nice hotel.

B: What did you do? ➜ A: I went surfing.

B: What did you see there? ➜ A: We saw the Sydney Opera House.

B: How was the scenery? ➜ A: It was amazing!

B: What did you eat there? ➜ A: We ate lobster.

B: What souvenirs did you buy? ➜ A: I bought koala toys.

LISTEN

A travel blog

🎧 DL 25   💿 CD 25

A Listen to a blogger talk about his recent trip to Cambodia. Put a check mark in the circles next to the correct picture.

Travel Blog
in Cambodia

How did he go?

Which month did he go?

06

07

Where did he visit?

🎧 DL 26   💿 CD 26

B Now listen to the rest of the blog. Complete the text below.

The tour guide picked me up _____ in the morning, so I could see

the sunrise. First, I climbed the main temple of Angkor Wat and took lots of

_____. The scenery was amazing.

Angkor Wat is a huge area with lots of different temples, so I was glad my tour guide had

his _____ to take me around.

Because a lot of the temples are in the _____, Angkor Wat is a really

mysterious place. The atmosphere was _____!

In Siem Reap, I bought some souvenirs for my _____. I bought some small

gifts from a temple and a _____.

READ MORE

C Then look at the mind map below. One of the pictures in each section is not in the blog. Listen to the whole of the blog and cross out the incorrect pictures.

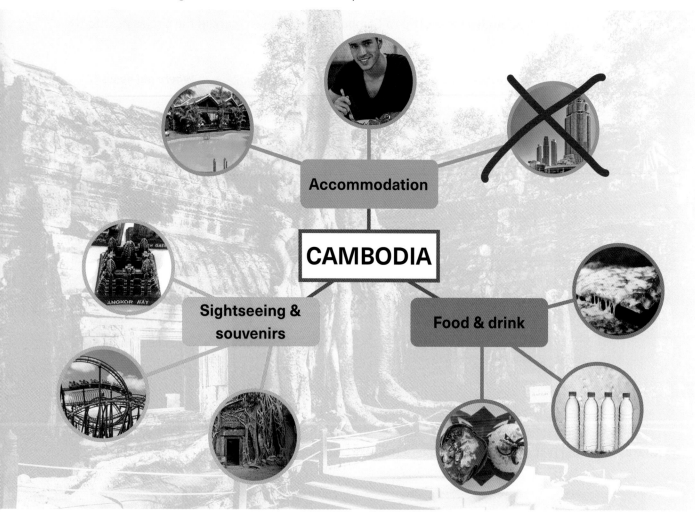

D 💬💬 Give your opinion!

1. I would like to see Angkor Wat.

Agree: _____   Disagree: _____

Why? _____

2. I would like to travel to many famous places abroad.

Agree: _____   Disagree: _____

Why? _____

3. What is the best form of transportation?

Answer: _____

Why? _____

4. When abroad, you should eat the local food.

Agree: _____   Disagree: _____

Why? _____

COMMUNICATE

What do you know about travel?

TRAVELOPOLY RULES

In groups of three or four, use a pencil, and without looking, touch one of the dice in the box. Check the number, move that number of spaces and answer the question or follow the instructions.

Did you go to an amusement park last year?

Who did you spend last New Year's holiday with?

Name the five countries at the beginning of Module 3.

Name the five countries at the beginning of Module 1.

Catch an express train, go forward 4 spaces

Did you travel anywhere by plane last year?

When was the last time you went on vacation?

Name the six countries at the beginning of Module 5.

Did you buy any souvenirs on your last trip?

Taxi gets a flat tire, go back 2 spaces

What did you do last summer vacation?

When did you last travel abroad?

Did you go skiing or snowbording last winter?

Name three countries in Europe beginning with the letter "S."

Oh no, miss the bus to the airport. Go back 5 spaces

Did you visit a temple or shrine on New Year's Day this year?

Did you go anywhere by ship or ferry last year?

Arrival

What was your best ever trip or vacation in Japan?

Long wait at immigration, go back 2 spaces

Disaster! You lose your passport. Go back to Departure

Did you go to a festival last year?

Where did you go on your high school trip?

Did you go anywhere nice in Golden Week?

Name four World Heritage Sites in Japan.

Did you go to the beach last year?

Name five capital cities in Asia.

Decide to stay an extra night. Skip one turn

Did you stay in a hotel last year?

What did you eat on Christmas Day last year?

A friend takes you sightseeing. Go forward 2 spaces

Departure

UNIT 12

READ / WRITE / VOCABULARY / LANGUAGE REVIEW

READ

Postcards and vacation reviews

A *Brainstorm:* Where did you go on your last trip in Japan / abroad? What did you do? How was the weather? What did you eat?

B *Pre-reading:* In pairs, partner (A) looks at the postcard on this page, partner (B) looks at the same postcard on the next page. Ask your partner for hints for the missing words.

| For example: | Partner (A): *Number 6.* |
| | Partner (B): *They are gifts that you buy when traveling.* |

Postcard from Hawaii

Partner A

Hi, how are you doing? I'm on vacation in Hawaii. I arrived two days ago. I ¹ _flew_ direct. The flight was good. It ² _____ six hours from Tokyo. On the first day, I went ³ _shopping_ at the Ala Moana Center. I ⁴ _____ some great beach ⁵ _shorts_ and ⁶ _____. After that, I ⁷ _ate_ dinner at a live music Cafe and I ⁸ _____ fresh pineapple ⁹ _juice_. The food was ¹⁰ _____. Yesterday, the ¹¹ _weather_ was very hot and sunny, so in the morning I went ¹² _____. In the afternoon, I went ¹³ _hiking_ and ¹⁴ _____ to the top of Diamond Head. The view was ¹⁵ _amazing_. Last night I ¹⁶ _____ to the hotel ¹⁷ _restaurant_ and ¹⁸ _____ Hawaiian food. The Kalua pork was so good.

I'm having a great time. You should come here! See you when I get back to Japan.

In pairs, partner (B) looks at the postcard on this page, partner (A) looks at the same postcard on the previous page. Ask your partner for hints for the missing words.

For example:　Partner (B): *Number 13.*
Partner (A): *Going for a long walk to enjoy nature.*

Postcard from Hawaii

Partner B

Hi, how are you doing? I'm on vacation in Hawaii. I arrived two days ago. I ¹_____ direct. The flight was good. It ² _took_ six hours from Tokyo. On the first day, I went ³_____ at the Ala Moana Center. I ⁴ _bought_ some great beach ⁵_____ and ⁶ _souvenirs_. After that, I ⁷_____ dinner at a live music Cafe and I ⁸ _drank_ fresh pineapple ⁹_____. The food was ¹⁰ _delicious_. Yesterday, the ¹¹_____ was very hot and sunny, so in the morning I went ¹² _swimming_. In the afternoon, I went ¹³_____ and ¹⁴ _climbed_ to the top of Diamond Head. The view was ¹⁵_____. Last night I ¹⁶ _went_ to the hotel ¹⁷_____ and ¹⁸ _tried_ Hawaiian food. The Kalua pork was so good. I'm having a great time. You should come here! See you when I get back to Japan.

C Read a tourist's review of their trip to Dubai. Complete the details on the mind map below about the accommodation, sightseeing and souvenirs, and food and drink.

 **D U B A I**

 Last year, I went on vacation to Dubai with my friends. We had an amazing time. We stayed in a really luxurious hotel. Our rooms were really big, and the hotel had three swimming pools. My room was on the top floor, and the view from my window was spectacular.

The weather in Dubai was really hot and humid, but I did a lot of sightseeing. We went to a waterpark which was so much fun. We went on lots of water rides, and I bought a souvenir t-shirt. My favorite part of the trip was taking a river cruise. We saw lots of beautiful temples, as well as the famous Burj Khalifa. It's the world's tallest building and was stunning. We didn't go to the top of the Burj, but we did take a helicopter ride and took some wonderful photos.

 The food in Dubai was really good. Our guidebook had some great advice on the best places to eat, so we went to some fantastic restaurants without needing to make reservations. The weather was hot in Dubai, so we ate inside during the day. At night we could enjoy eating outside. There was a lot of ethnic food to choose from, and I enjoyed eating Indian food the most. I ate different types of curries with naan bread. It was delicious!

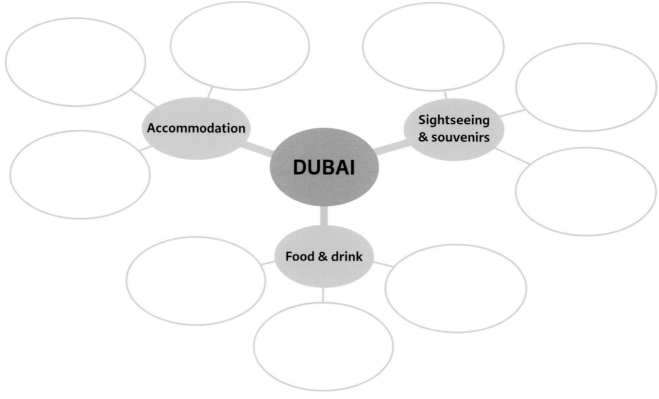

WRITE

Your trip

A *Word check:* Complete this review of a camping trip to Miyazaki. Use words from the vocabulary box below to help you.

Last _____, I went camping the countryside in Miyazaki with my friends. It was _____! We stayed at a great camp site. The _____ was beautiful. It was next to a really nice _____, and there were lots of people surfing. Our tent was nice too. It was big and _____.

We saw a lot of beautiful nature. There was a big mountain near the campsite. So, in the mornings, we ate breakfast and then went _____. In the afternoons, we went to the seaside and _____ on the beach. The _____ was hot! We also went cycling, which was a lot of fun. There was a great gift shop near the campsite, so I bought some nice souvenirs for my family.

The food in Miyazaki was _____. We bought food and drinks at the local supermarket, then we cooked everything ourselves. In the evenings, we had a _____. We cooked sausages, chicken and pork. We also cooked fresh fish. Then, in the mornings, we cooked _____ and drank tea. It was a lot of fun!

> beach   summer   delicious   weather   relaxed(×2)
> hiking   comfortable   scenery   fantastic   barbecue

B *Writing skill:*

> ### Mind mapping
> Mind mapping can help you plan your ideas in a clear way before you start writing. First, think of the main ideas that you want to write about. Then think of supporting details or examples and link them together. When you have finished, your mind map will show you all the information you need to write about in a clear way.

C *Let's Practice:* Think of a trip you had in Japan or abroad. Complete the mind map below by giving examples about the accommodation, sightseeing and souvenirs, and food and drink.

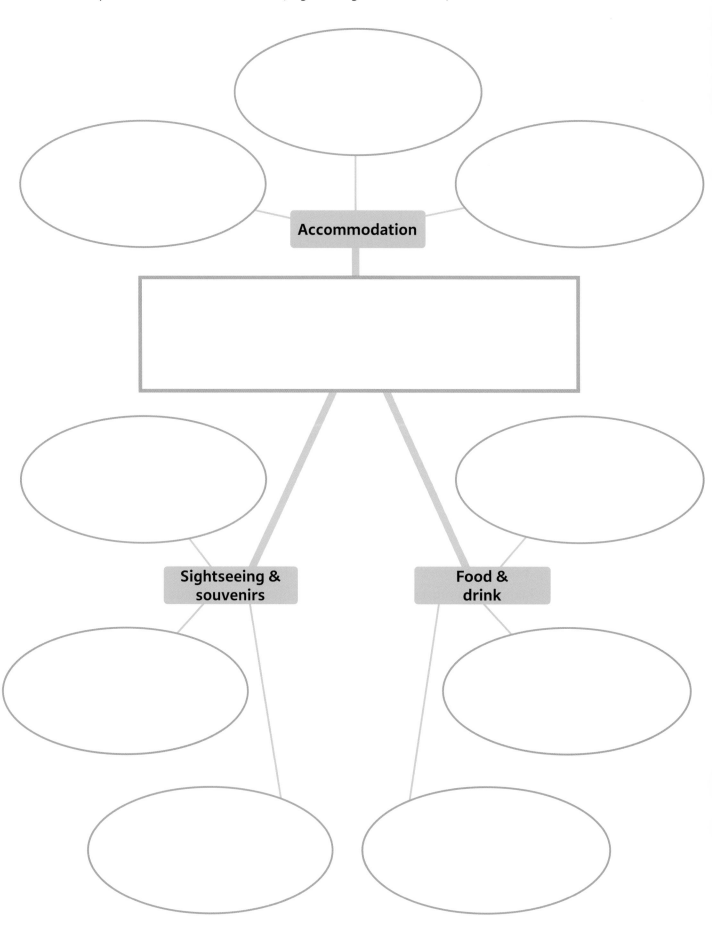

D *Task:* Use your mind map to help you write about your trip. Write three short paragraphs:

Paragraph 1: *Where did you go? How was the accommodation?*

Paragraph 2: *What did you see there? What souvenirs did you buy?*

Paragraph 3: *How was the food and drink?*

My Trip

VOCABULARY

DL 29   CD 29

Adjectives

amazing *B1* ....
fantastic *A2* ....
humid *B1* ....
local *A2* ....
luxurious *B2* ....
spectacular *B1* ....
stunning *B1* ....
wonderful *A1* ....

Nouns

accommodation *B2* ....
airport *A1* ....
amusement *A2* park *A1*
....
arrival *B1* ....

atmosphere *B1* ....
backpacking *B1* ....
baggage *B1* ....
beach *A1* ....
bus *A1* ....
camping *A2* ....
castle *A2* ....
cathedral *B2* ....
check-in *B1* ....
countryside *A2* ....
cruise *A2* ....
customs *B1* ....
departure *B1* ....
destination *B1* ....
flight *A2* ....
guidebook *A2* ....

holiday *A1* ....
hiking *A2* ....
homestay *＋* ....
hostel *B1* ....
immigration *B1* ....
journey *A2* ....
luggage (baggage) *B1* ....

passport *B1* ....
reservation *B1* ....
scenery *A2* ....
shrine *＋* ....
sightseeing *A2* ....
souvenir *B1* ....
temple *A1* ....
tour *A2* ....

tourist *A2* ....
transportation *B1* ....
trip *A1* ....
vacation *A1* ....
view *A2* ....
weather *A1* ....

Verbs

arrive *A1* ....
drive *A2* ....
fly *A1* ....
stay *A1* ....
take *A1* (a train *A1*) ....
travel *A1* ....
visit *A1* ....

A Match each definition with the words on the right.

1. Visiting interesting places as a tourist: _____
2. Form of travel from place to place: _____
3. A gift bought on vacation: _____
4. The place where passports are checked: _____
5. Suitcases and other bags used to carry your things while traveling: _____

a. luggage (baggage)
b. souvenir
c. transportation
d. sightseeing
e. immigration

B Cross out the word that does NOT belong in the list.

At the airport:	immigration	customs	countryside	check-in
Vacation:	holiday	trip	tour	cathedral
Accommodation:	baggage	hotel	homestay	hostel

C Choose the words from the box that best complete the questions. Answer the questions.

beach   backpacking   weather   stay   souvenirs

1. What ☐ did you buy on your last trip?   A: _____
2. How was the ☐ last weekend?   A: _____
3. Did you go to the ☐ last year?   A: _____
4. Would you like to go ☐ sometime?   A: _____
5. When did you last ☐ at a hotel?   A: _____

94

D *Crossword:* Complete the crossword using the hints below.

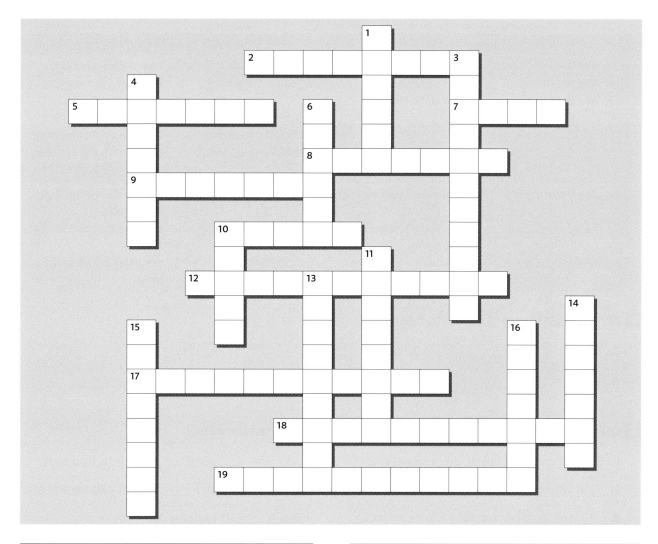

Across

2. I bought a koala toy as a _____ .

5. How was the _____ ? Terrible! It rained all day!

7. Where did you _____ ? At a nice local hostel.

8. The mountain _____ was so beautiful. I took lots of photographs.

9.

10.

12.

17.

18.

19.

Down

1. I think Kiyomizu-dera is the most famous _____ in Japan.

3. That restaurant is really popular. You need to make a _____ .

4.

6.

10. Summer is so hot and _____ in Japan.

11. Where did you go on your last _____ ?

13. I bought a great _____ . It had lots of advice on local restaurants and the best places to visit.

14. The train _____ takes about 1 hour.

15.

16.

LANGUAGE REVIEW

Past tense questions (Be verb)		Past tense Wh- questions (Other verbs)	
How was the weather?	It was cloudy.	What did you do?	I went backpacking.
How was the hotel?	It was really nice.	Why did you like it?	The scenery was amazing.
How was the food?	It was delicious!		
		Where did you stay?	We stayed at a hostel.
		When did you arrive?	We arrived on Tuesday.
		Who did you go with?	I went with my brother.
Yes/No questions (Be verb)		**Yes/No questions (Other verbs)**	
Was your vacation fun?	Yes, it was. I had a great time.	Did you enjoy the flight?	Yes, I did. The service was good.
Was the weather cold?	No, it wasn't. It was quite warm.	Did your wife like the food?	Yes, she did. She loved it.
Was the food tasty?	Yes, it was. I loved the fresh pasta.	Did they have a good time?	Yes, they had a great time.

A Write the past tense of the verbs below.

1. fly _____   **2.** take _____   **3.** stay _____

4. visit _____   **5.** travel _____   **6.** drive _____

B Complete the questions, then match them with the completed answers.

1. Where _____ your family go on vacation? •   • Yes, she _____. She _____ some stuffed toys.

2. _____ your sister buy any souvenirs? •   • It _____ beautiful. I _____ a lot of photographs.

3. _____ the weather sunny? •   • No, it _____. It rained a lot.

4. How _____ the scenery? •   • They ___ to Hawaii. They _____ a great time.

C Put the answers in the correct order. Match the answers with the questions.

1. Did you buy a souvenir last vacation   [   ]   **a.** [Kyoto / went / I / to]

_____

2. Where did you go on holiday last year?   [   ]   **b.** [yes / went / in / I / shrine / Narita / to / a]

_____

3. Where did you eat lunch yesterday?   [   ]   **c.** [I / didn't / go / no / shopping]

_____

4. Did you stay at a hotel last year?   [   ]   **d.** [ate / the / in / I / lunch / hotel / restaurant]

_____

5. Did you visit a shrine last month?   [   ]   **e.** [didn't / I / no / . / I / hostel / stayed / in / a]

_____

MODULE 5 SELF-CHECK

Write a score (1-5)* in the boxes below to show how well you can do each part of the module. If you can't do any part well, go back to the page and practice again.

* 1 : Not at all   **2 :** A little   **3 :** OK   **4 :** Well   **5 :** Very well

UNIT 11

SCAN
I can scan for information about famous places (p.83). ·····················

FOCUS
I can describe my past vacations or trips (p.84). ·····················

LISTEN
I can understand a travel blog about a vacation (p.85-86). ·····················

COMMUNICATE
I can answer questions about travel (p.87). ·····················

UNIT 12

READ
I can read and understand postcards and vacation reviews (p.88-90). ·····················

WRITE
I can write about a trip I had (p.91-93). ·····················

VOCABULARY
I can understand vocabulary related to travel (p.94-95). ·····················

MODULE 6

Rules

GOALS:

 Can you scan for information about rules around the world?

 Can you describe rules in Japan and around the world?

 Can you understand a lecture about rules at a university?

 Can you answer questions about rules and customs around the world?

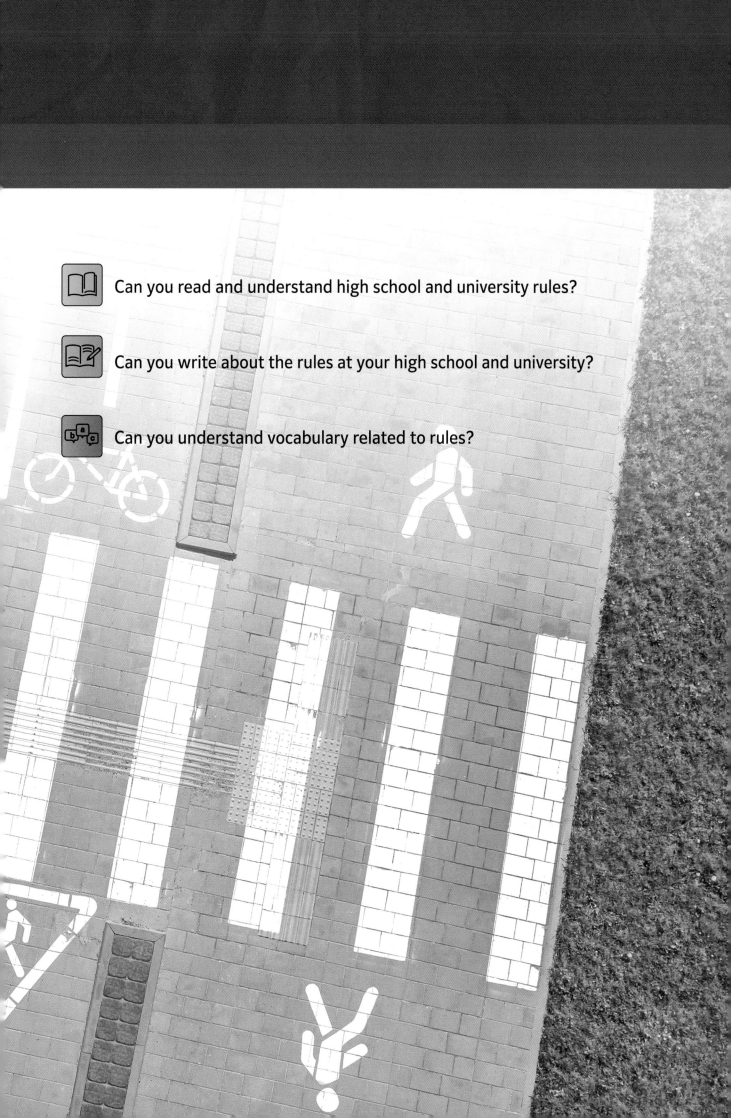

Can you read and understand high school and university rules?

Can you write about the rules at your high school and university?

Can you understand vocabulary related to rules?

MATCH

Look at signs **1-6**. Try to guess which signs match pictures **a** - **f** below. Write the letter in the space next to the signs below.

SCAN

Rules around the world

 DL 30  CD 30

A *Scanning for information:* In 4 minutes, scan the texts below to find the key information. Check your answers on the previous page.

B Read the texts again and write the name of the place(s) you usually find these signs in the correct space on the previous page.

1.

You can walk dogs on the beach, but in places where you see this sign, you must keep your dog on a leash. You mustn't let your dog run around freely, because it might disturb other people. Also, please clean up after your dog!

In South-east Asian countries, you can see these signs in hotels, airports, shopping centers and on public transportation, such as buses. You mustn't take durian fruit into any place where you see this sign because durians have a very strong smell.

2.

3.

You are not allowed to camp where you see this sign. This sign means that this place is not a campsite, so you mustn't put up tents here. You often see these signs on private land, national parks and mountain areas.

If you see this sign, you must slow down and drive carefully to avoid traffic accidents. It means there are wild animals in this area. There are many different animal warning signs all around the world, but you only see this kangaroo sign in Australia.

4.

5.

A brown sign represents leisure information. This sign means that people can have picnics here. There are usually special picnic areas in parks. But, remember, you must take your garbage home with you.

A red circle with a red line across it is used to warn people of something they are not allowed to do. This sign means that people mustn't talk loudly. You usually see this sign in libraries and other places where you should speak quietly.

6.

C In pairs, discuss what rules or customs in Japan you think are important for foreign visitors to know.

FOCUS

A *Rules:* Match phrases **1-6** with pictures **a**-**f** below.

1. You **can't** drink alcohol under 20 years of age. ⸱⸱⸱⸱⸱⸱⸱⸱⸱⸱⸱⸱⸱⸱⸱⸱⸱⸱⸱⸱⸱⸱⸱⸱⸱⸱⸱⸱⸱⸱⸱⸱⸱⸱⸱⸱⸱⸱ ☐

2. You **must** take off your shoes when entering someone's house. ⸱⸱⸱⸱⸱⸱⸱⸱⸱⸱⸱⸱⸱⸱⸱⸱⸱⸱⸱⸱ ☐

3. You **have to** score a goal to win! ⸱⸱ ☐

4. You **can** wear casual clothes. ⸱⸱⸱ ☐

5. You **mustn't** use your phone when driving. ⸱⸱⸱⸱⸱⸱⸱⸱⸱⸱⸱⸱⸱⸱⸱⸱⸱⸱⸱⸱⸱⸱⸱⸱⸱⸱⸱⸱⸱⸱⸱⸱⸱⸱⸱⸱⸱ ☐

6. You **don't have to** shake hands in Japan. You can bow. ⸱⸱⸱⸱⸱⸱⸱⸱⸱⸱⸱⸱⸱⸱⸱⸱⸱⸱⸱⸱⸱⸱⸱⸱⸱ ☐

a.

b.

c.

d.

e.

f.

B *Rule questions:* Match the questions below with phrases **1-6** as the answers.

What is a Japanese custom when entering a house? ( )	What is a Japanese custom when meeting someone for the first time? ( )
What is one of the rules of soccer? ( )	What is the dress code at university? ( )
What is a rule for driving? ( )	What is a rule for drinking alcohol in Japan? ( )

C 💬💬 *Let's talk:* In pairs, practice asking questions about rules in Japan, then give rules or suggestions..

For example:

A: What are the rules for this course?   B: You must ... / You have to ... / You mustn't ...

A: What are the rules when travelling on a train?   B: You mustn't ... / You have to ... / You can't ...

A: What are the rules in a library?   B: You can't ... / You have to ... / You mustn't ...

LISTEN

A lecture about class rules

 DL 31 CD 31

A Listen to the first part of a lecture. Put a check mark next to the correct circles below.

Who is talking?	*Where are they?*	*What subject?*

DL 32 CD 32

B Now listen to the rest of the lecture. Complete the text below.

First, please make sure that you attend your classes. You must attend _____ of your classes to pass.

Second, you can use _____ in class. They can be used as dictionaries so that's OK.

But you mustn't _____ in class. However, drinking water, tea or soda drinks is fine.

And for your English classes, please try to _____ English. You don't have to speak English all time, but try to speak English to your teacher and your classmates.

Follow these rules to help you _____ your classes.

C Now listen to the whole of the lecture. Put a check next to the correct pictures.

University Rules			
Obligation (must / have to / had to)	**Attend class**		
	50% ☐	60% ☐	70% ☐
Permission (can / could)	**Cell phones**		
	☐	☐	☐
Prohibition (musn't / can't / couldn't)	**Food**		
	☐	☐	☐
Prohibition (musn't / can't / couldn't)	**Library**		
	☐	☐	☐

D 💬💬 Give your opinion!

1. Students should be allowed to use cell phones in class.

Agree: _____   Disagree: _____

Why? _____

2. University students should wear uniforms.

Agree: _____   Disagree: _____

Why? _____

3. All university students must study English

Agree: _____   Disagree: _____

Why? _____

4. Students mustn't be late for morning classes.

Agree: _____   Disagree: _____

Why? _____

COMMUNICATE

What does your partner know about rules and customs around the world? (Partner A)

Read the following rules to your partner. Write your partner's guess (true or false) in the table. Check your partner's score using the answers below. (Correct=1 point)

Rules	True / False
1. People in India mustn't eat chicken. Birds are holy animals for Hindus.	
2. You mustn't touch people on the head in Thailand. It is very rude.	
3. In Switzerland, you will get a fine if you don't recycle your garbage.	
4. In South Korea, men have to do military service.	
5. It is illegal to feed pigeons on the streets of San Francisco.	
6. In New Zealand, you can't start driving until you are 21.	
7. You are not allowed to bring chewing gum into Singapore.	
8. In Spain, you can't drink alcohol if you are under the age of 21.	
9. Students in Quebec, Canada must be taught in French.	
10. You have to drive on the left in Ireland.	
Total number of correct answers:	

ANSWERS: 1. false (but beef is banned as cows are holy animals) 2. true 3. true 4. true 5. true 6. false (you can start driving at 16) 7. true 8. false (the legal drinking age is 16) 9. true 10. true

Assessment result

10 points	You are an expert on international cultures and customs. Perhaps you should become a diplomat in the future. Or maybe you cheated!
7-9 points	You know a lot about different rules and customs around the world. You are interested in learning about cultural differences.
4-6 points	Although you do know some things about the rules and customs of different countries, you should read more about different cultures.
1-3 points	There is more to the world than staying at home! You should open your eyes and learn more about the world around you.
0 points	Really?! Zero?! No points at all! I guess you don't like traveling!

COMMUNICATE

What does your partner know about rules and customs around the world? (Partner B)

Read the following rules to your partner. Write your partner's guess (true or false) in the table. Check your partner's score using the answers below. (Correct=1 point)

Rules	True / False
1. Women are not allowed to join the army in Israel.	
2. In Australia, you don't have to tip in restaurants.	
3. You mustn't eat with your right hand in Indonesia. You should use your left hand.	
4. In Italy, you should drink cappuccino in the morning, not in the afternoon.	
5. In Sweden, you have to drive with your lights on even during the day.	
6. In China, you should give clocks or shoes as gifts at a wedding.	
7. Women have to cover their heads and arms when they enter a mosque in Egypt.	
8. You mustn't give the "OK" sign to someone in Brazil. It is very rude.	
9. In some historic places in Greece, such as the Acropolis, you can't wear high heels.	
10. You have to show your passport when traveling from England to Scotland.	
Total number of correct answers:	

ANSWERS: 1. false 2. true 3. false (it's rude to eat with your left hand) 4. true 5. true 6. false (they are bad luck) 7. true 8. true 9. true 10. false (both England and Scotland are part of the UK)

Assessment result

10 points	You are an expert on international cultures and customs. Perhaps you should become a diplomat in the future. Or maybe you cheated!
7-9 points	You know a lot about different rules and customs around the world. You are interested in learning about cultural differences.
4-6 points	Although you do know some things about the rules and customs of different countries, you should read more about different cultures.
1-3 points	There is more to the world than staying at home! You should open your eyes and learn more about the world around you.
0 points	Really?! Zero?! No points at all! I guess you don't like traveling!

READ
High school and university rules

A *Brainstorm:* Do you agree, or disagree, with your school rules (taking tests, wearing a school uniform, using phones in class)?

> **For example:** *I don't agree with wearing a school uniform because it doesn't give the students a chance to express themselves.*

B *Pre-reading:* Write high school and university rules **1-8** next to the correct pictures below.

at high school	at university

1. I couldn't wear make-up or jewelry.

2. I can wear casual clothes. I don't have to wear a uniform.

3. I couldn't use my phone in the classroom.

4. I have to cook my own dinner in the evening.

5. I had to wear a school uniform.

6. I have to do lots of homework and assignments.

7. We had to clean the school every evening before we went home.

8. I don't have to wake up so early every day.

C Read a student's experience of high school and university. Find two more rules for high school and university that are different from the previous page, and write them in the blank spaces on the previous page.

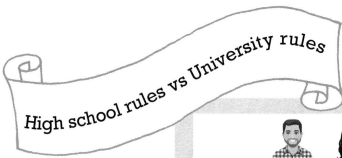

High school rules vs University rules

At my high school, there were many rules. I woke up at 6:00 a.m. every day because classes started between 8:00 – 8:30 a.m. I had to wear a school uniform. I didn't like my uniform because it was boring. Girls weren't allowed to wear make-up or jewelry. I had to take a bus to school because it was far from the train station. I could bring my phone to school, but I wasn't allowed to use it in class. At lunch, we all had to eat in the school cafeteria. I didn't like the meals because there wasn't much choice. Finally, after school, I had to take extra English classes three times a week. I had to do a lot of homework to pass all the tests. High school was very tiring!

At my university the rules are different. I like being a university student because I don't have to wake up early! My apartment is next to the university. I also don't have to wear a uniform. I love wearing casual clothes! My major is International Business. I have to attend lots of classes, and I mustn't be late for class. I have to get 60% to pass my English classes, but I want to get over 80% so I can get an "A" grade! I can eat my lunch at the cafeteria, but I don't like the food there. I try to cook my own food, but I have no time because I have a part-time job. I work most evenings at a convenience store. I finish at 10:00 p.m. so I have no time to cook my dinner. I want to find a different part-time job, so I have more free time.

WRITE

A *Word check:* Complete the passage below. Use words from the vocabulary box to help you.

At my high school, there were many rules. I _____ at 7:00 a.m. every day. I couldn't

be _____ for class. I had to wear a uniform. There were tests every week. I had to study a lot of

English. For example, I had to _____ lots of new words every week! I also couldn't use

my _____ in class. My teacher was very _____. We always had to follow her _____.

At my _____ the rules are different. I don't have to wear a uniform, I can wear _____

clothes! I have to attend lots of classes. I only have _____ tests during the semester, but I also

have a lot of writing _____, and there are lots of tests at the end of the semester. For club

activities, I _____ to a tennis club. We play tennis twice a week. I also have a part-time job.

I work at a convenience store during the week until 10:00 p.m., but I can go home _____ on

Tuesdays.

belong	a few	casual	rules	memorize	late
phone	assignments	woke up	university	early	strict

B *Writing skill:* Narrative paragraph writing

❯ Narrative writing is about writing a story. The story could be about things that have happened to you over time.

   For example: *writing about your high school days.*

❯ A narrative paragraph starts with a topic sentence followed by supporting details.

   For example: I *really like university. I don't have to wake up early every day!*

❯ A narrative can be about you so make sure to use "I / my ..."

C *Let's Practice:* write about the dress code at your high school and university.

At my high school _____

I _____

At my university _____

I _____

D *Task:* Are the rules at your high school and university similar or different? Write two paragraphs. Think of topics to write about, for example:

- Dress code
- Classes / English study
- Eating food
- Club activities

For example:

Paragraph 1: *Write about the rules at your high school (use the past tense).*

Paragraph 2: *Write about the rules at your university (use the present tense).*

Check READ on page 107-108 as a guide but use your own ideas! Remember to use a main idea and supporting details for each paragraph.

Rules

VOCABULARY

DL 35 CD 35

Adjectives		far *A2*		homework *A1*		Verbs	
absent *B1*		(a) few *A2*		jewelry *A1*		allow *A2*	
illegal *A2*		loudly *A2*		law *A2*		attend *B1*	
legal *B1*		most *A2*		make-up *A2*		belong *A2*	
private *A2*		quietly *A2*		mosque *A2*		borrow *A1*	
public *B1*				obligation *B2*		bow *B2*	
rude *A1*		**Nouns**		permission *A2*		disturb *A2*	
similar *A2*		assignment *B1*		phone *A1*		fail *A2*	
strict *A1*		custom *A2*		prohibition *B1*		follow *A2*	
Adverbs/Determiners/ Pronouns		dress code +		rule *A1*		memorize *B1*	
		experience *A2*		semester *A2*		pass *A2*	
carefully *A1*		fine *B1*		traffic *A2*		prohibit *B2*	
early *A1*		garbage *A1*		accident *A2*		wake (up) *B1*	

A Match each definition with the words on the right.

1. Instructions that tell you what you can and can't do: _____
2. Traditional or usual ways of doing things: _____
3. Give permission to do something: _____
4. Spring or fall period at university: _____

    a. semester
    b. customs
    c. rules
    d. allow

B Write a word with the opposite meaning to the words listed below.

1. public ⟷ _____
2. pass ⟷ _____
3. legal ⟷ _____
4. loudly ⟷ _____
5. prohibit ⟷ _____
6. be absent ⟷ _____

C Choose the words from the box that best complete the questions. Answer the questions.

course   dress   library   alcohol   driving

1. What is the [_____] code at university?   A: _____
2. What is a rule for drinking [_____] in Japan?   A: _____
3. What is a rule for [_____] in Japan?   A: _____
4. What is a rule for this [_____] ?   A: _____
5. What are the rules in a [_____] ?   A: _____

D *Crossword:* Complete the crossword using the hints below.

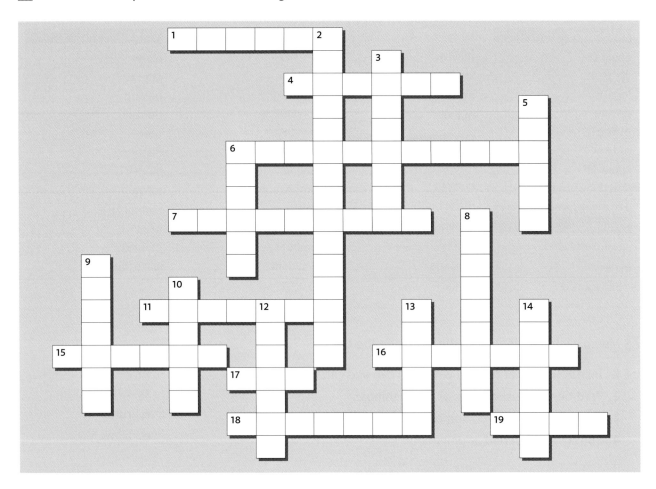

Across

1. My mother is so _____ . We have lots of rules at home.

4.

6. I have to do a lot of writing _____ for homework.

7. We don't have a _____ at university. We can wear casual clothes.

11.

15. I _____ my driving test last week. I'm very happy.

16.

17. (image of two people bowing)

18.

19. You must study hard or you'll _____ the English test.

Down

2. (image of car crash)

3. I _____ to the volleyball club at high school.

5. (image of mosque)

6. I was _____ from school because I had a cold.

8. We have two _____ at university, spring and fall.

9. Did you go to a public or _____ high school?

10. I always _____ at 6:30 a.m. in the morning.

12. I wasn't _____ to stay up late when I was a child.

13. (image of man shouting)

14. In Japan, it is _____ to drink alcohol unless you are over 20.

LANGUAGE REVIEW

Explaining laws, rules and customs

Prohibition - present tense (mustn't, can't)	Prohibition - past tense (couldn't)
You mustn't be absent from class a lot. You can't park your car here.	My sister couldn't wear make-up at high school. When I was a child, I couldn't stay up late.
Obligation - present tense (must, have to)	**Obligation - past tense (had to)**
Do we have to buy a text book? You must finish your assignment this week.	She had to wear a uniform in high school. My brother failed the test, so he had to take it again.
No obligation - present tense (don't have to)	**No obligation - past tense (didn't have to)**
He doesn't have to wear a tie at work. I don't have to work tomorrow.	I didn't have to make dinner last night. My friend cooked. They didn't have to get up early last Sunday.
Permission - present tense (can)	**Permission - past tense (could)**
Can I go to the toilet, please? You can sit here.	At school, I could only use my phone after class, not during lessons.

A Choose the modal verb that best completes the sentences.

1. You _____ drive over 100 km/h on expressways in Japan.   [have to / can't]
2. Yesterday, she _____ write two assignments.   [had to / mustn't]
3. In Japan, you _____ drink alcohol if you are under 20.   [can't / must]
4. When I was 15, I _____ go to bed early on weekends.   [didn't have to / mustn't]
5. You _____ only smoke in special smoking areas.   [mustn't / can]
6. You _____ tip in restaurants in Japan.   [don't have to / have to]

B Match the questions with the correct answers.

1. Do I have to turn off my phone in class?   •   • Of course you can. Here you are.

2. Can I borrow your pen?   •   • No, I didn't. I started at junior high school.

3. Could your sister go to the concert?   •   • No, you don't, but use the silent mode.

4. Did you have to study English at elementary school? •   • Yes. My mother gave her permission.

C Match the signs with the rules.

1.   •   • You have to stop.

2.   •   • You can't eat or drink here.

3.   •   • You mustn't take photographs here.

4.   •   • You can park here.

MODULE 6 SELF-CHECK

Write a score (1-5)* in the boxes below to show how well you can do each part of the module. If you can't do any part well, go back to the page and practice again.

* 1 : Not at all   **2 :** A little   **3 :** OK   **4 :** Well   **5 :** Very well

UNIT 13

SCAN

I can scan for information about rules around the world (p.101). ⬝⬝⬝⬝⬝⬝⬝⬝⬝⬝⬝⬝⬝⬝⬝⬝⬝⬝⬝

FOCUS

I can describe rules in Japan and around the world (p.102). ⬝⬝⬝⬝⬝⬝⬝⬝⬝⬝⬝⬝⬝⬝⬝⬝⬝⬝⬝⬝⬝⬝

LISTEN

I can understand a lecture about rules at a university (p.103-104). ⬝⬝⬝⬝⬝⬝⬝⬝⬝⬝⬝⬝

COMMUNICATE

I can answer questions about rules and customs around the world (p.105-106). ⬝⬝⬝⬝⬝⬝⬝

UNIT 14

READ

I can read and understand high school and university rules (p.107-108). ⬝⬝⬝⬝⬝⬝⬝⬝⬝⬝

WRITE

I can write about the rules of my high school and university (p.109-110). ⬝⬝⬝⬝⬝⬝⬝⬝⬝⬝

VOCABULARY

I can understand vocabulary related to rules (p.111-112). ⬝⬝⬝⬝⬝⬝⬝⬝⬝⬝⬝⬝⬝⬝⬝⬝⬝⬝⬝⬝⬝⬝⬝⬝⬝⬝

PROJECT E

What are popular places to take a trip in Japan?

Ask 10 students with the questions below about their best trip in Japan. Find out reasons for students answers.

INTERVIEWS (Best Trip in Japan)

	Where did you go?	Why did you like it?	What did you do?	What did you eat there?	What souvenirs did you buy?
1					
2					
3					
4					
5					
6					
7					
8					
9					
10					
Comments					

REPORT

Write about any similarities or differences in your results. Try to use main ideas and supporting details.

For example: *University students enjoy different trips in Japan. For example, three students went to Okinawa, three students went to Kyoto, two students went to Niigata and two students went to Osaka.*

PRESENTATION

In groups, explain the results of your interviews to your classmates.

PROJECT F

What rules are important for a Japanese university?

Ask 10 students their opinion about the following rules:

1. All students must study English.

	Strongly agree	Agree	Depends	Disagree	Strongly Disagree
Number					
%					

2. All class sizes must be small (max 20 students per class).

	Strongly agree	Agree	Depends	Disagree	Strongly Disagree
Number					
%					

3. All students must study a language in a foreign country for at least three months.

	Strongly agree	Agree	Depends	Disagree	Strongly Disagree
Number					
%					

4. English should be taught by both Japanese and foreign teachers at university.

	Strongly agree	Agree	Depends	Disagree	Strongly Disagree
Number					
%					

5. Classes should have Japanese and foreign students studying together.

	Strongly agree	Agree	Depends	Disagree	Strongly Disagree
Number					
%					

6. All classrooms must have computers or students must use tablets.

	Strongly agree	Agree	Depends	Disagree	Strongly Disagree
Number					
%					

7. The cafeteria must serve healthy Japanese and international food for students.

	Strongly agree	Agree	Depends	Disagree	Strongly Disagree
Number					
%					

RESULTS

Based on the percentages on the previous page, draw pie charts to show your data.

For example:

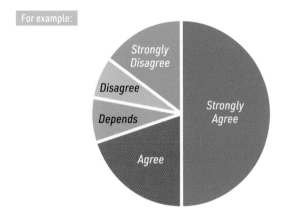

1. All students must study English.

2. All class sizes must be small.

3. All students must study a language in a foreign country for at least three months.

4. English should be taught by both Japanese and foreign teachers at university.

5. Classes should have Japanese and foreign students studying together.

6. All classrooms must have computers or students must use tablets.

7. The cafeteria must serve healthy Japanese and international food for students.

REPORT

Write the results of your survey and think of reasons to explain the results.

For example:
- *Eighty percent of students strongly agree that all students must study English. Students must study English because it is the world language.*

PRESENTATION

In groups, present your results to your classmates.

Image Credit and Sources

p.44   Pelmeni (Milena Pivinskaya)

Hoppers (Mideki Fernando)

p.86   Angkor Wat in Cambodia © Zoom-zoom|Dreamstime.com

Framework English A (CEFR A1-A2)

CEFRの評価基準で学ぶ4技能 A (CEFR A1-A2)

2024年1月20日　初版第1刷発行
2024年2月20日　初版第2刷発行

著　者　Colin Thompson
　　　　Tim Woolstencroft

発行者　福　岡　正　人

発行所　株式会社　金星堂

（〒101-0051）　東京都千代田区神田神保町3-21
Tel　（03）3263-3828（営業部）
　　　（03）3263-3997（編集部）
Fax　（03）3263-0716
https://www.kinsei-do.co.jp

編集担当　長島吉成　　　　　　　　　Printed in Japan
印刷所・製本所／株式会社カシヨ

ISBN978-4-7647-4200-0　C1082

MODULE

SELF-CHECK

for submission

MODULE 1 SELF-CHECK

Write a score (1-5)* in the boxes below to show how well you can do each part of the module. If you can't do any part well, go back to the page and practice again.

* **1 :** Not at all   **2 :** A little   **3 :** OK   **4 :** Well   **5 :** Very well

UNIT 1

SCAN
I can scan for information about nationalities (p.7). ⋯⋯⋯⋯⋯⋯⋯⋯⋯⋯⋯

FOCUS
I can introduce myself and ask personal questions (p.8). ⋯⋯⋯⋯⋯⋯

LISTEN
I can understand people when they introduce themselves (p.9-10). ⋯⋯⋯

COMMUNICATE
I can ask and answer personal questions about other people (p.11-12). ⋯⋯⋯

UNIT 2

READ
I can read and understand introduction messages (p.13-14). ⋯⋯⋯⋯

WRITE
I can write a message introducing myself (p.15-16). ⋯⋯⋯⋯⋯⋯⋯

VOCABULARY
I can understand vocabulary related to introductions (p.17-18). ⋯⋯⋯⋯

ID: _____   Name : _____

MODULE 2 SELF-CHECK

Write a score (1-5)* in the boxes below to show how well you can do each part of the module. If you can't do any part well, go back to the page and practice again.

* 1 : Not at all   **2 :** A little   **3 :** OK   **4 :** Well   **5 :** Very well

UNIT 3

SCAN

I can scan for information about fashion styles (p.23).

FOCUS

I can describe my fashion interests (p.24).

LISTEN

I can understand a conversation about clothes (p.25-26).

COMMUNICATE

I can find out about my classmates' fashion styles (p.27).

UNIT 4

READ

I can read and understand people's opinions about fashion (p.28-29).

WRITE

I can write my opinion about the clothes I like (p.30-31).

VOCABULARY

I can understand vocabulary related to fashion (p.32-33).

ID : _____ Name : _____

MODULE 3 SELF-CHECK

Write a score (1-5)* in the boxes below to show how well you can do each part of the module. If you can't do any part well, go back to the page and practice again.

*1: Not at all   2: A little   3: OK   4: Well   5: Very well

UNIT 6

SCAN
I can scan for information about food from different countries (p.45). ⋯⋯⋯⋯⋯ ☐

FOCUS
I can discribe my eating habits (p.46). ⋯⋯⋯⋯⋯⋯⋯⋯⋯⋯⋯⋯⋯⋯⋯⋯ ☐

LISTEN
I can understand a restaurant review (p.47-48). ⋯⋯⋯⋯⋯⋯⋯⋯⋯⋯⋯ ☐

COMMUNICATE
I can ask and answer questions about eating habits (p.49). ⋯⋯⋯⋯⋯ ☐

UNIT 7

READ
I can read and understand restaurant menus and restaurant reviews (p.50-51). ⋯⋯⋯ ☐

WRITE
I can write a restaurant review (p.52-53). ⋯⋯⋯⋯⋯⋯⋯⋯⋯⋯⋯⋯⋯ ☐

VOCABULARY
I can understand vocabulary related to food (p.54-55). ⋯⋯⋯⋯⋯⋯⋯ ☐

ID:＿＿＿＿＿＿＿＿＿＿＿   Name:＿＿＿＿＿＿＿＿＿＿＿

MODULE 4 SELF-CHECK

Write a score (1-5)* in the boxes below to show how well you can do each part of the module. If you can't do any part well, go back to the page and practice again.

* 1 : Not at all   **2 :** A little   **3 :** OK   **4 :** Well   **5 :** Very well

UNIT 8

SCAN

I can scan for information about lifestyles (p.61). ⋯⋯⋯⋯⋯⋯⋯⋯⋯⋯⋯⋯⋯⋯⋯⋯⋯⋯

FOCUS

I can describe my lifestyle using adverbs of frequency (p.62). ⋯⋯⋯⋯⋯⋯⋯

LISTEN

I can understand a lifestyle podcast about diet, exercise and sleep (p.63-64). ⋯⋯⋯⋯

COMMUNICATE

I can talk about my health and lifestyle (p.65). ⋯⋯⋯⋯⋯⋯⋯⋯⋯⋯⋯⋯⋯⋯⋯⋯

UNIT 9

READ

I can read someone's description of their diet, exercise and sleep (p.66-67). ⋯⋯⋯⋯

WRITE

I can write about my diet, exercise and sleep (p.68-69). ⋯⋯⋯⋯⋯⋯⋯⋯⋯⋯⋯

VOCABULARY

I can understand vocabulary related to lifestyle (p.70-71).⋯⋯⋯⋯⋯⋯⋯⋯⋯⋯⋯⋯

ID:＿＿＿＿＿＿＿＿＿＿＿   Name:＿＿＿＿＿＿＿＿＿＿＿＿

MODULE 5 SELF-CHECK

Write a score (1-5)* in the boxes below to show how well you can do each part of the module. If you can't do any part well, go back to the page and practice again.

* 1 : Not at all   **2 :** A little   **3 :** OK   **4 :** Well   **5 :** Very well

UNIT 11

SCAN
I can scan for information about famous places (p.83). ·······························

FOCUS
I can describe my past vacations or trips (p.84). ·······························

LISTEN
I can understand a travel blog about a vacation (p.85-86). ·······························

COMMUNICATE
I can answer questions about travel (p.87). ·······························

UNIT 12

READ
I can read and understand postcards and vacation reviews (p.88-90). ·······························

WRITE
I can write about a trip I had (p.91-93). ·······························

VOCABULARY
I can understand vocabulary related to travel (p.94-95). ·······························

ID : _____   Name : _____

MODULE 6 SELF-CHECK

Write a score (1-5)* in the boxes below to show how well you can do each part of the module. If you can't do any part well, go back to the page and practice again.

* 1 : Not at all   **2 :** A little   **3 :** OK   **4 :** Well   **5 :** Very well

UNIT 13

SCAN
I can scan for information about rules around the world (p.101).

FOCUS
I can describe rules in Japan and around the world (p.102).

LISTEN
I can understand a lecture about rules at a university (p.103-104).

COMMUNICATE
I can answer questions about rules and customs around the world (p.105-106).

UNIT 14

READ
I can read and understand high school and university rules (p.107-108).

WRITE
I can write about the rules of my high school and university (p.109-110).

VOCABULARY
I can understand vocabulary related to rules (p.111-112).

ID:＿＿＿＿＿＿＿＿＿＿＿＿＿   Name:＿＿＿＿＿＿＿＿＿＿＿＿＿